Caren Ann & Ron

Dedicated to

Caren Ann Jackson

I had friends in Albuquerque who moved to Salem, Oregon, sometime in 1999. Elaine and Alex Sanchez were the most engaging couple. Elaine was the Sales Manager at the CBS station in Albuquerque. Alex was the head of Central New Mexico Community College. One day I walked into Elaine's office, and she told me she was getting married. I said, "Who is the lucky fella"? She responded, "Alex Sanchez." I blurted out, "Alex Sanchez at the community college here? I know him"!

Elaine said, "Why didn't you introduce me to him earlier. He is a terrific guy, and we're getting married next month."

Less than a year later, Elaine called me one evening while I was working in my office. After a few minutes of "How are you?" chatter, she said, "Would you like to meet the woman I think you will marry?"

I am in Albuquerque; she is in *Oregon* . . . Somewhat perplexed ...I replied, "WHAT? "Elaine, please let me speak to Alex."

Alex took the phone and said, "Listen to Elaine. This woman is a wonderful, beautiful, resourceful person. Well worth meeting." Alex's recommendation kept me on the phone.

Eventually, after some months of phone calls, cards, and emails with Caren Ann, I flew to Portland to meet her. I learned that she had been hired as the first executive director of Salem's hand-carved, one-of-a-kind Riverfront Carousel, completed in 2001. She had worked with Hazel Patton to organize, fundraise, and oversee construction of the world-class attraction, now named in Hazel's honor.

Caren Ann met me at the airport, and I realized quickly that she was beautiful, resourceful, and a great person. She was also skilled in creating conversations. During this first get together, she had plans to go to her hometown of Nyssa, in eastern Oregon.

The occasion was to pack up her parents' household belongings and assist their move to the west side of the state. This also gave me the opportunity to meet her seven siblings and their spouses. Like Caren, the rest of her family was bright, engaging, and genuinely nice to me. Her parents, Wilton and Margery, were very welcoming, as were her five sisters, two brothers, and spouses.

I did not realize this at the time, but over the next 21 years, I would spend a lot of time with Wilton and Margery. They moved to Mary's Woods in Portland, a very nice retirement center. Spending time with her parents, it struck me that I have spent a lot more time with my in-laws than those in my family of that same generation.

Wilton and Margery died a few days apart over the Valentine's Day holiday a couple of years ago. He was 100 years old, and Margery was 93. Both were extremely vital over the last few years of their lives.

During those 21 years, we spent many holidays visiting them at Mary's Woods. Christmas, Thanksgiving, Easter, birthdays, and reunions were a part of the celebration of family.

Caren Ann was the second born and Lynn Marie was the first child. They were born in Temple, Texas, and Caren Ann, to this day, claims Texas as her birthplace. Texas has never been a sacred place for me. It sure is big and has wonderful people, but it also has the most undistinguished criminal justice system in the country.

Next came Marcia, followed by Bruce, the first of the two boys. The rest of the children, in order of birth, were Nancy, Jill, Megan, and Tom. All of them are wonderful people, married to outstanding spouses, and raising youngsters.

Caren Ann not only blessed me with her large biological family, but a second family as well, this being the Red Door Community. The goal of this large group of interesting and diverse individuals is to do nice things for other people. Its leader for the 20-plus years that I have been involved has been Lani O'Callaghan. "Do-Good" activities include helping members who need a "Red Door Day," whether it is for yard work, delivering meals to someone ill or laid up, running a garage sale, moving, celebrating, or grieving. Red Door membership ranges in age from 80+ years to teenagers. Over the past number of years, members have passed, and funerals have been attended. Most of the funerals were certainly celebrations of life… Life as a member of Red Door.

During our time together, and before I came on the scene, Caren Ann has been deeply involved in almost every aspect of Red Door activity.

She has organized many Red Door volunteer events, as well as participated in nearly all of them. One of her strong points is hard work. It doesn't matter who it is, those in need find a helping hand from Caren Ann, Lani, and so many of the others. Among the many charitable things that Lani and Caren Ann do is support refugees from all around the world as they resettle in Salem. This has been a source of joy for her; she says that she gets back more than she gives.

Caren Ann has also been involved with many of the organizations that I've associated with, and has taken on speaking roles on my behalf in the past couple of years. Here are just some of those organizations that she has helped me with: Oregonians for Alternatives to the Death Penalty, Let's Dance, cooking food and serving meals to the homeless, and visiting incarcerated members of our society, where we have tried to elevate their dignity and self-worth.

Caren Ann has a wide circle of friends, some of them since high school, and some of them new. At first, we tried to live half a year in New Mexico and half a year in Salem. We found that it was difficult to deal with and expensive to maintain. During the six months each year in New Mexico, she found new friends, some of whom I had never known before. Some of her friends there have stayed in touch over the telephone and occasionally visited our home in Oregon, as we did theirs in New Mexico. Caren Ann has such ease and authenticity when it comes to meeting people. She has brought many great people into my life.

I consider myself lucky, having followed up on Elaine and Alex's introduction. Caren Ann has been a wonderful partner and lover. She gracefully involved herself with many of my projects and, just as gracefully, engaged me with hers. She is beautiful on the inside and outside. We share a similar Catholic faith, which has been important to me throughout my life.

We have also traveled to some exciting places, both in this country and abroad. Ever eager, if you name a town or city and say something nice about it, she will want to go there. Our life together has been wonderful, but in all honesty, not perfect. We are different in several ways. She is more social than I. She befriends almost everybody; I'm more introverted, yet we are always on the same team.

My declining condition has been challenging for us. Caren Ann has been by my side through the best times and the toughest times. She has hired great caregivers to help us both during this time. Our differences aside, the love we have for one another is unmatched. I love you, Caren. Thank you for our partnership. I will be with you as long as I possibly can, and possibly beyond that too!

seek PEACE.
give SERVICE.
be HAPPY.

seek PEACE.
give SERVICE.
be HAPPY.

———

ISBN: 979-8-9899066-1-1 - *softcover*
ISBN: 979-8-9899066-0-4 - *hardcover*
ISBN: 979-8-9899066-2-8 - *ebook*

———

Book Design & Production
timmyroland.com

seek PEACE.
give SERVICE.
be HAPPY.

ron STEINER

GIRAFFE

TABLE *of* CONTENTS

TABLE *of* CONTENTS

Be Happy.

Testimonials

Epilogue

seek PEACE.
give SERVICE.
be HAPPY.

PROLOGUE

I hope that you will enjoy reading this collection of recollections. I have been pondering these stories for a long time, some of them for more than 20 years.

I'd like to share credit for this compilation with friends and family members who, in the process, have taught me many things about writing and organizing a memoir. Among them are Tim Buckley and Paul Patton, who have been valuable in terms of story selection and editing. About the look and feel of the book, the design, and getting it to publication, added thanks goes to Tim Gilman.

My son Michael and daughter Amy have been remarkably encouraging and helpful with this memoir - reading, editing, and proofreading the stories, many of them multiple times. But their impact began a long while before I started writing. It was they, decades ago, who encouraged me to work less, travel less, and to do more volunteering. Many of these stories would not have been possible without their kind coaxing and, more recently, their advice.

Amy, at age six or seven, started working on me to quit smoking. Now in her middle years - a mom, author, business owner, and a licensed clinical social worker, Amy is still providing me valuable counsel on many things.

Michael, also in midlife, is a dad, a prestigious academy administrator and educator, who has earned accolades in this country and abroad for his vision of excellence and his passion for helping young people find their bright path in the world.

You'll read in these pages a bit of my own vision and passions, many of which revolved around recognizing talent in other people and then giving them tools with which to be more successful, whether that be at developing markets, inspiring sales staffs, or helping non-profit organizations to raise money, pass legislation, or better serve the communities they represent.

All the people in these stories have been wonderful for me to know, folks with great energy and committed values. They have, in turn, helped me stay positive, focused, and committed to values as well.

A wise man once told me, "If you don't tell the important stories of your life, they will die before you do." I'm happy to have taken his advice.

INTRODUCTION

What is a memoir?

According to the Google dictionary, a memoir is a historical account or biography written from personal knowledge. Synonyms include: accounts, histories, records, stories, and reports of people who have contributed to one's life.

Some consider memoirs a chance to enhance a life story without the "fact checkers" hovering. Others consider memoirs to be lightly embellished accounts, written without malice but fashioned to appear more interesting.

Seek Peace, Give Service, Be Happy is a nonfiction book, colored only by my memories of what really happened along the roads of life. This is my effort to share a story of a life well-lived, of lessons learned, and of lessons shared as I attempt to follow a mantra: "seek peace, give service, be happy."

This is not a chronological biography. Rather, it is a series of articles offered to share stories and honor inspirational people who have contributed to my life. Among the articles are life memories, personal letters, essays, answers to interesting questions, and profiles. All of them are offered as ideas and guidance to inspire and help people to seek peace, give service, and be happy.

This letter from April 2, 2020, is an example of how I tried to connect old stories to my mantra. At the time, Covid was raging, and I was in Salem with Caren Ann.

Dear Sister Bernice

I wish I could handwrite this letter, but that skill has passed me by since learning in the third grade with Sister Consolata at St. Bernard's School.

I hope that my feelings and emotions come through the keyboard.

The concern with Coronavirus is no April Fools joke. My prayers and best wishes are with you as I think of you and others in my circle of friends.

Without this tumult affecting every aspect of life, Caren and I would be in Albuquerque this week to attend and celebrate the Italian Film Festival, and visit friends there. Alas, no trip, no festival, no visiting. Hunkering down in Salem, Oregon, trying to make wise decisions.

With Caren's daughter and son-in-law being nurses, and my son-in-law having been director of health in a nearby county, we have received plenty of cautionary lectures on how people our ages should behave. I might have been a little cavalier about the whole thing, but no longer.

Can you believe, or even imagine, the dispensation of Holy Mass, let alone Holy Week and Easter Mass not being available? I am sure God understands, and the Holy Spirit is providing counsel to those in the church calling the shots.

One of the ways that I am using my time during this "stay put" period is working on a book. Once I passed age 80, I started to think seriously about writing a memoir. At first, I found it too self-serving and conceited.

I have served on a lot of boards over the years -- Habitat for Humanity, Futures for Children, the Italian Film Festival (a benefit for The UNM Childrens' Hospital), the New Mexico Coalition to Repeal the Death Penalty, and Oregonians for Alternatives to the Death Penalty.

While my book will include some chapters about my family and stories of people who influenced me, I hope it shows more humility than a straightforward memoir.

You are someone I would like to include in the profiles of the book, if only briefly.

I distinctly remember the first day we met, at the front door of Our Lady of the Garage (early name for Prince of Peace.) You were selling raffle tickets to win a new car from Casey Luna's Ford dealership. That must have been in the mid-to-late 80's. You were powerfully successful at selling.

Since that first encounter, the Holy Spirit always seemed to tip you off when I had some cash in my pocket to support whatever you were selling. I loved being a friend of someone so close to the Holy Spirit.

For the book, I have a couple of pieces about Father Mondragon. His sermon on forgiveness has guided me ever since I first heard it. All my correspondence now ends with a salutation - "Peace." That comes from him, wishing us "peace of mind."

Although we will view Easter Mass on television, may all its blessing reach out to you just as fully.

Peace,

Ron

PS: The change of address card is evidence that it was time for me to get into a place all on one floor, and for us to "downsize."

Son of a Butcher

I am a son of a butcher. My dad owned a little butcher shop and neighborhood grocery store. When I was in second grade, I had my first job working in the store. My dad was a very hard-working guy; he made sure the family was well fed, had the essentials we needed, and felt safe. He worked in the store six days a week and, on Sundays, he did bookwork and painted signs for the next week's specials: for eggs, or roasting chickens, or bologna for 39 cents a pound.

Me as an infant, well fed and nearly cleaned up.

As children, my siblings and I did not learn to fish, hunt, camp out, or have a family vacation each year. We did, however, learn how to work.

As a college graduate, a husband and father, my youthful lessons became a part of me. My job, my focus, my purpose, and my passion, was to provide for my family.

That focus on hard work served me and my family well during 40-plus years spent in sales, marketing, and management in the commercial television industry. At some point in my early 60's, it came to me that I needed to get beyond defining myself merely as hard working and smart. Instead of working solely for personal and my family's interests, I began to focus on making the rest of the world a better place.

That led me into serial community service – dedicated and creative work, not for money but rather to serve others: Habitat for Humanity, Futures for Children, the University of New Mexico Children's Hospital, the New Mexico Italian Film Festival, and then the Dismas House.

The Dismas House, a transition house for formerly incarcerated men and women, then led me to volunteer for the New Mexico Coalition to Repeal the Death Penalty—my path to leadership in mission-driven organizations.

A move to Oregon connected me to Oregonians for Alternatives to the Death Penalty, where I continued to labor happily, full time, to make a difference. My most recent endeavors have been raising money to provide temporary shelters for the homeless of Salem, and creating a series of fundraiser dances at Salem's Riverfront Park.

Community service organizations are populated by caring, loving, wonderful people. But, they're not necessarily folks with a background in marketing. Success in any non-profit volunteer organization depends on understanding the marketing process. Like selling beer, shoes, cars, or fashion, it is all about marketing.

From one non-profit to the next during my trek through community service, I would hear things like, "We can't do that," or, "We never did that before," or, "How could we do that without a budget?" Many of these organizations were not doing what they needed to do to thrive. They were frozen in history and fear. I would always return to my roots in hard work and entrepreneurship. The starting line was always: "Let's try it. We can't fall off the floor."

Thanks to my foundation and formation as the son of a butcher, I always enjoyed hard work. Whether working to create success for corporations that employed me, working to provide for my family, or working for the common good, I have found fulfillment, enrichment, and fun.

The Best Job I Ever Had

I have had lots of jobs, from low-paying ones as a youngster, to my volunteer jobs as an adult and senior citizen.

Only a few of those jobs were lousy, for me and the employer. Notable among this small group of losers was the first real job I secured right out of college. I was hired in Pittsburgh as a credit investigator for Dunn & Bradstreet. I had an assigned territory in southwestern Pennsylvania, West Virginia, and southeast Ohio.

The job was to travel that territory, update previous credit reports and write reports for new businesses. The worst aspect was that I had to ask people how much money they were making. In my upbringing, that type of personal information was kept private. I quit before the first year was up.

Then I went to work for my brother as a manufacturers' rep in architectural sales, representing two product lines, trying to get architects to "spec" curtain walls and church pews. Sadly, I did not even know how to read specs or blueprints. I quit after a year, once again a failure. Or so I thought at the time.

One of my more enjoyable early jobs was as a sales rep with the Colgate Palmolive Company. I was assigned to the Pittsburgh territory and part of the enjoyment was my trainer/managers - Tazwell Hobgood and Jim Slaney. My next regional manager was Jim Sweeney, first in the Syracuse area and then in Washington DC. At Colgate Palmolive, I really learned how to sell.

I left Colgate Palmolive to go to law school at Duquesne University. I was taking night classes and worked days for Pittsburgh Beer, loading and unloading trucks in their warehouse. As luck would have it, I flunked out of law school.

My next sales job (Shulton, Inc.) was selling Old Spice products designed for men. At Old Spice, and at Colgate, my car trunk was always full of product samples. My family and friends loved those jobs as much as I did.

Then I was hired by Tony Renda at WIIC-TV in Pittsburgh, selling television advertising. As a local salesperson, calling on businesses and advertising agencies, I took to it easily.

My strategic plan for advancement was to get a promotion in five years. I started at WIIC-TV, Channel 11, in August of 1966. In the first five years, I was promoted to local Sales Manager. In another five years, I became the General Sales Manager. By the next five year mark, I had resigned and taken a job as General Manager at the ABC affiliate in Toledo, WDHO-TV. So eager to become a GM, I did a poor job of researching my new boss, station owner Daniel Over-meyer. He had no morals when it came to business practices, so I quit after five months.

Within a month, I was offered the GM position at a new independent station, KLKK-TV, in Albuquerque. The work was challenging and required creativity. I did well. But, after two years the owner, Eddie Peña, fired me. Sad and hurt at the time, it turned out that Eddie did me a huge favor.

The next job would become my very BEST, as founder and CEO of Marketing Communications Group, as a consultant to TV station owners. I remained in that job from 1982 until my retirement in 2008.

"Retirement" really should be defined as the end of work for pay. Starting in 1992, I started to do non-profit volunteering. My first role was as unskilled labor – doing tasks for Habitat for Humanity, helping to build houses.

That started a series of non-profit volunteering. After Habitat for Humanity there was Futures for Children, The Dismas House, New Mexico Coalition to Repeal the Death Penalty, New Mexico Children's Hospital, Murder Victim Families for Reconciliation, and Oregonians for Alternatives to the Death Penalty. The tasks ranged from hammering nails to stuffing envelopes, from writing letters to creating marketing plans, from serving on boards to chairing two different boards. While building my own business was so pleasurable, giving my free labor through these various non-profits was every bit as rewarding.

How I Started My Own Business

Running my own business was the best career move I ever made. Creating something is a way of finding peace. As is the case with most good things, I owe a lot to the wonderful people who helped me.

Fifteen years working for television stations gave me a good foundation to take further steps, under the auspices of the Marketing Communications Group. I was very blessed and lucky to have worked with people who cared about and appreciated me. The first break came from Dick Noll.

Dick had a successful career working for national manufacturers of food products. Campbell Soup was among them. Dick started his own consulting company and developed something that became known as "vendor support marketing."

While I was the local sales manager at WIIC-TV in Pittsburgh, Dick's partner, Roland Eckstein, would come into one or more of their client's markets two or three times a year, for three or four days at a time. Our job as a sales team was to set up appointments with retailers that had a common position in the market, as well as sellers of name brand products. It was almost magical, the way retailers responded to these presentations, learning that there is additional funding for advertising beyond regular co-op plans.

Noll & Company was on a roll, helping retail clients. They created valuable campaigns that increased sales, based on tactics detailed in the action plan.

As a local TV sales manager in Pittsburgh, I would tag along on client calls, listening intently, and learning the presentation by heart. The strategy was a "win-win" for everybody. The retailers who paid attention to Dick's plan got a profitable promotion, developed by an experienced consultant and paid for by the television station, not the client. The television station also got a happy advertising client, who became a loyal ad buyer.

Years later, when managing the station in Albuquerque, I got a call from Dick, who wanted to expand his roster of TV station clients. Based on his positive experience with me in Pittsburgh, he thought that I was ideal to join their organization. I accepted his generous offer, and we continued in business for many, many years. In 1982, my business, Marketing Communications Group, became an affiliate of Noll & Company.

To start me off, Dick assigned me four stations. I served as consultant to WTSP TV in Tampa/St Pete, the two McGraw-Hill stations in Denver and San Diego, and the CBS affiliate in Phoenix.

Beyond those first four TV stations, I was then given free rein to recruit additional stations. With my experience in Pittsburgh and Dick's coaching, it was easy for me to sign up additional stations in Lexington, Albuquerque, Sacramento, San Antonio, and Tucson.

The basic product we offered to stations was called vendor support work, which was very lucrative for the stations. The success of Noll's program led my developing a consultancy in other, tangential areas that were also popular and lucrative.

It had become evident to me that sales training was lacking in most every station I visited. So, I launched a sales training business. Dick had no problem with my that, because I was still making lots of money for him with their vendor support service program. Over the next 20 years, training salespeople and sales managers became a major part of my consultancy to TV stations.

My consulting and training academy began in the 1980s and, for more than 20 years, I taught hundreds of young sales and marketing people, many of whom became ad execs, marketing experts, and station managers around the country.

Training salespeople at TV stations had always been the domain of the in-house sales managers. Sales managers got their jobs because they were the best sellers, not necessarily the best trainers.

Based on my experience hiring and training salespeople, I developed a comprehensive sales training program and made it available exclusively to broadcast TV stations.

In the first years as a consultant to station management, I built trust and continued to produce innovative ideas for making them more money. Revenue for the stations also became revenue for me. From salespeople to sales managers to station managers, and all the way up to corporate decision-makers, my team worked hard to earn trust.

While working on behalf of KGUN-TV in Tucson, I found one of their station projects was a winner for them. I secured permission from their management to take this successful campaign to other stations. The campaign was complex but a sure winner.

Salespeople would go to their advertisers and prospective advertisers, offering them a profitable position in a coupon book that would be published in the upcoming months, Using the coupon books with their ads inside, together with the TV station's broadcast schedule, it drove the retailer's customers to use the coupons and tune into the TV station, where the retailer's ads would be airing. It was a win for customers, who would save on retail products and services. It was also a win for retailers and for TV stations.

In the next two years, I was able to place that identical strategy into fifty different markets across the country. All I had to do was recruit the stations then turn most of the coupon work over to the printing company, who would deal directly with retailers and the stations. This was another revenue stream for Marketing Communications Group.

Next, based on the trust that I had established, and my connections with upper management throughout the country, I offered station managers a comprehensive audit of their sales department. My audit covered all aspects of selling and inventory management.

The audit included a two-day visit to the TV station where I interviewed all managers, salespeople and the department heads. From these interviews, I could usually find some areas of excellence and I could always find areas of need. The audit report was 20 to 30 pages of analysis and recommendations.

The report was delivered to sales managers and general managers, and eventually worked its way up to the management and owners, hence adding the potential for more effectiveness and profit for the company.

My second lucky break was when Jack Sander, the GM at my Phoenix station, moved up the corporate ladder of the Belo Company, headquartered in Dallas, Texas. The Belo Company started as a newspaper publisher and, at the time, owned The Dallas Morning News, one of the most respected and profitable newspapers in the world. More important to me, the Belo Company owned twelve or thirteen TV stations around the country. Jack became president of that division of Belo.

It was early December of 1999. I was flying back from doing a presentation to the Georgia Broadcast Association, walking through the Atlanta airport, and by total chance, met Jack on his way to catch a flight of his own.

Jack was in a hurry to catch his flight, but also eager to share some conversations that he recently had with Paul Karpowitz, the vice president of LIN television company, and Tony Vincaquarra, Vice President of sales for Hearst broadcasting company. The three companies collectively owned 38 outstanding television stations around the country. Their conversations were about sales training. They had the concept that a school should be developed to provide new salespeople with the skills to sell successfully in the television industry.

In his haste to catch his flight, Jack said "I have an opportunity for you and trust that you are the person that can put this together. I'll call you next week with more details."

The promised call from Jack came early the next week. More calls between the three principals took place that week as well.

This was the genesis of the Broadcast Sales Academy.

The concept that Jack laid out, speaking for the other two companies as well, was a school for the brightest new hires at the stations. They would be invited to a month-long school held at the Belo headquarters in Dallas.

I was delighted to have the opportunity to develop the curriculum, the timetable, and the instructors who would join me in implementing the plan. I would handle about 60 to 70 percent of all lesson plans.

Some of the lesson plans I developed included strategic selling, building trust, customer service, business and television math, account list management, negotiations, and establishing relationships as a basis for customer allegiance, something to generate repeat business for many years because of good relations.

I made a presentation to Jack, who shared it with Paul and Tony. I got a positive response almost immediately. The first Broadcast Sales Academy training took place in the hot Dallas summer of 2000.

Jack, Paul, and Tony introduced the two people who would take care of all the housekeeping details in Dallas. They became wonderful partners in the endeavor. Sherry Brennan and Lucy Dettl were both on the Belo management staff and were priceless in helping execute a smooth first edition of Broadcast Sales Academy.

Broadcast Sales Academy (BSA) was my absolute best "gig" ever.

The population of each BSA class was close to 30 people and the students were outstanding hires for the companies. BSA got better with each session, which carried on for me through 2007.

By 2007, the overall business of the Marketing Communications Group had grown, and I was getting weary from too many nights away, too many hotel rooms, too many airplane flights, and too many restaurant meals. It was time to start winding down my business.

An Idea Ahead of Its Time

Being a consultant to television stations and their retail advertisers provided an inside look at a lot of different businesses. Being the son of a butcher, I always was interested in the retail business. After all, I started to work in my dad's store when I was in second grade and continued throughout high school and even during college years. In high school, I worked every Saturday and after school each day, except when I was practicing on the football or basketball teams.

One of the first TV stations that Dick Noll turned over to me to handle was WTSP-TV10 in Tampa – St. Petersburg, Florida. I would visit the market three or four times a year, for a few days - making calls on retailers to share the retail/advertising strategy that Dick had perfected. The station salespeople and sales managers were to identify retailers that carried a lot of nationally-branded merchandise and had a major presence in their retail category. I was the "drummer," the consultant from out-of-state, who would explain the strategy and, if convinced it was a fitting way to expand business on the vendor's nickel, the station would assign me to help the retailer employ the strategy, solicit the vendors, and set up the media/marketing plan for growth.

On one of my initial trips into the market, Frank Ratterman, one of the station's account executives (a fancy name for salesperson) identified a retailer that he seemed to think was a good prospect. The retailer (with just one outlet and no real presence in the market) was not a good prospect for our strategy. Additionally, the products they sold were not all famous brand names, and some of their vendors were trying to find another type channel of distribution from the (then) typical reseller of office supplies. But Frank and I made the call anyway to see what we could learn and practice my "pitch", which was still in the developing stages.

The retailer, this many years later I cannot remember the name, was in fact a single outlet, but in a very large space, formerly a supermarket of 25,000 to 30,000 square feet. The traditional supermarket shelves gave way to large metal racks that soared toward the ceiling. Stacks and stacks of office supplies of all sorts, all at reduced prices, highlighted with blazing bright signage screaming "50- 70% OFF" discounts.

These prices were killing traditional office supply retailers. Most office supply stores had a store front, but much of their business went out the back door, into trucks that delivered products to customers' places of business. Pricing was set by the retailer, with the only discount given at the end of the year. "Buy more, earn more on your rebates" was a simple, straight-forward business angle. The competition among re-sellers was based on one's breadth-of-inventory to meet business' needs, as well as superior customer service, and the year-end rebates.

The incidental sales of pens, notebooks and ring-binders, for school supplies or home use, was never discounted and never amounted to a significant percentage of the resellers' total revenue.

Although this was not a prospect for our trail-blazing strategy (see the previous chapter about Dick Noll) seeing the store sparked an idea for me. Never had I seen such a retail outlet and it fit with some of the reading I was doing about the changes in our society and the impact of those changes on business. History will record that in 1982, John Naisbett made a contribution which changed the world, with his book Megatrends. Naisbett shifted the way we think about the world. He changed the way we think about ourselves.

In *Megatrends*, Naisbitt identified ten trends that would influence the future. While many of these seem now obvious and pervasive, few of them were evident in 1982:

- Becoming an information society after having been an industrial one
- From technology being forced into use, to technology being pulled into use because of its appeal to people
- From a national economy to one in the global marketplace
- From short term to long term perspectives
- From centralization to decentralization
- From getting help through institutions like government to self-help
- From representative to participatory democracy
- From hierarchies to networking

- From a northeastern bias to a southwestern one

- From seeing things as "either/or" to having more choices.

This was the pre-Internet era. This was a time that home offices were just starting to make sense to workers and businesses alike. This was a time that societal changes were budding. This was a time with major department stores that were unique to a market. It was before the department store consolidation that began with May Company and Federated Department stores, before they began to gobble up locally controlled retailers, market by market. Kaufman's in Pittsburgh, Meier and Frank in Portland, Foley's in Houston, Zion Stores in Salt Lake City, all of these eventually flew the May Company flag. Federated Department Stores, the corporation, was doing the same thing, and they aquired May Company in 2005. Supermarkets also started the same strategy, like the Kroger Company, which began in Cincinnati, acquired local, controlled food retailers across the land, under the Kroger flag.

Back to the "spark of an idea" . . . after leaving the market on my trip to Tampa/St. Pete, I could not get the image of racks of office products being sold at unheard of discount prices. When I returned to Albuquerque, I tried to develop a new retail concept for the Southwest, although it really couldn't be considered new, since I saw it in its embryonic state in Tampa. I worked it over in my mind then onto paper. But, this time, the paper came out of a dot-matrix printer attached to a desktop computer with a "floppy drive," just to remind you about the dawning of a new era.

I worked it around as best I could and shared the concept with my best buddy and neighbor Hal Hudson. Hal thought it was an innovative idea and came up with the perfect name: BusinesSmart.

A new name and concept were hatched and I set out to market it in Albuquerque, not exactly the epicenter of business innovation. My idea went beyond just office supplies, adding office furniture and a copy shop (ages before Kinkos). There was more than one of each of these businesses in Albuquerque and I went to visit the owners of the top-ranked businesses in each category.

My concept was to put the three businesses under the same roof, a former supermarket site. I would be the landlord and they would lease space to operate the aspect that they already knew best.

My first stop was with Mike Belew, at Belew's Office Products. He thought I was nuts. "No way do I need to discount," and out the door I flew with him kicking at my BusinesSmart presentation booklet.

Next, I trotted to Office Furniture Outlet with the same enthusiasm and, sadly, a similar result.

With my chin still high, I visited Bill Baxter at Alphagrapics, who said, "We are in the printing business, not the retail office supply business." "No thanks, Ron" At least Bill was nice about it, as opposed to my first two stops, both of whom were appalled at the idea.

I did my printing at Bill and Judy Baxter's shop for many years. They had a sign on the wall, behind the counter that was prominent enough for all to see, reading:

[*best* PRODUCT. *best* SERVICE. *best* PRICE. PICK TWO.]

So, to end this chapter of my creativity, BusinesSmart went out of sight before seeing the light of a retail day. Mind you, this was 1982.

To bring you up to date, the first Staples store was opened by Tom Stenberg, in 1985. The first Office Depot was opened in 1987. The first Office Max store was opened by Bob Hurwitz in 1988.

In 2014 Office Max and Office Depot merged. By that time, Belew's Office Products, the Office Furniture Outlet and Alphagraphics were left in the dust and out of business.

In retrospect, BusinesSmart was an idea ahead of its time and an example of a life lesson learned (perhaps more important than learning your ABCs): If you believe strongly in something, have the courage to stick with it as long as humanly possible. (Initial failure is just an opportunity to refine the idea and try again.) This can be especially valuable to non-profits that are trying to raise money or awareness.

Speaking Up - The Time Squeeze Scandal

Early in the 21st century, digital technology gave TV stations the ability to "squeeze" programming, so that viewers didn't realize they were getting at least one more 30 second ad each half hour. The practice at CBS cheated everyone but station executives. Below is a protest letter I wrote to CBS CEO Mel Karmazin, appearing in a 2001 edition of Electronic Media, a major trade journal for the industry.

We all now know what Mel Karmazin's favorite bird is. DUCK!

The CBS chief has been conspicuously absent from the pages of the trades since the news that his network affiliates have been caught squeezing programming to stuff even more commercials into their logs. It strikes me as odd that this man, who has "led" the network to "profitability" with his boisterous and boastful rhetoric, has ducked all queries about the spot CBS stations are now in.

Although prudence has kept employees of the Big Eye Network from speaking publically about the enormous pressure that Mr. Karmazin and his policies have placed on the CBS sales organizations, it is well known that it is ungodly pressure. If one thinks the programs have been squeezed, so have the salespeople and managers.

Over my more than 35 years in the business, I have worked with many CBS managers and salespeople. I know them to be good, hardworking, creative, thoughtful and basically honest people. But the pressure that has been put to bear on their collective shoulders has forced them to compromise the integrity of CBS and our industry.

Although I do not agree that it is at all proper, I can understand how CBS owned and operated station sales managers could do this to achieve the unrealistic demands coming from 51 W. 52nd St. They have mortgages to pay, families to feed and kids to send to college. What has happened, though, is these hard-driven men and women, who go home at night and teach their kids not to lie, cheat or steal, have done just that in the name of feeding the greed and ego of these directives.

The practices that have been uncovered have cheated the program producers by violating their contracts and changing the program content as it was delivered to the network for airing. They have cheated the advertisers, who are told of one set of standards and are then placed in commercial breaks unlike their description. They have cheated the viewers by cramming even more commercial clutter into their viewing. They have cheated their affiliates, who were forced to play by different rules than the CBS-owned stations. They have cheated their televeision station competitors in their respective markets, who have been faced with unfair competitive pressure, forcing rates down by overextending inventory in their markets. And worst of all, they have cheated themselves. They have sullied anyone associated with these stations who have worked so hard to practice their profession in an honest and fair manner.

We have constantly hammered away at the promise that professionals can be trusted. As a trainer of young salespeople, what do I tell these young people now?

Don't duck Mr. Karazin, leaving all good CBS employees to clean up the mess that has been created with the undue pressure to achieve your quotas.

Ron Steiner, Consultant and broadcast sales trainer,
Albuquerque, NM

Resignation From Television

If peace of mind means a sense of tranquility, we can surely use some peace when it comes to big changes in life. Below is the letter I sent to my business partner upon deciding to resign from the television industry. A sense of peace can also come when we reflect on how much the world has changed over the years.

Dear Gary,

Jan. 4, 2014

I hope that you and your wonderful family had a very blessed and joyful holiday season. I thought of you often over the past few weeks, surrounded by children and grandchildren in your big Vista house, all smiles and happiness.

I have been thinking of you in anticipation of writing this letter. I want you to know how truly grateful I am that you came into my life and have taken a business that I nurtured for many years and have made it even better. After 47 years in the television business, the time has come for me to end that segment of my life.

When I started at WIIC-TV, the NBC affiliate in Pittsburgh, in August of 1966, there were just three television networks. Television stations were predominately owned by small companies, newspaper companies or individual owners. The top shows in 1966 were The Lucy Show, Bonanza, Gunsmoke, Andy Griffith, and Dean Martin specials.

Lyndon Johnson was President and Hubert H. Humphrey was the VP. Life expectancy was 70.2 years. Baltimore defeated the Dodgers in the World Series, Texas Western (with five Black players) defeated Adolf Rupp and the all-white Kentucky Wildcats in the NCAA basketball championship. The Viet Nam War continued to be a divisive issue in our country. The US homicide rate was 5.9 per 100,000 adults, and I started off in an industry I knew nothing about. I had no idea what would unfold.

Today it is a very different world, a very different television industry and a much different media complex … one that is passing me by.

It is time to close that chapter of my life. I do so with great confidence that you will continue the training that I cared so much about in a very distinguished fashion. I like to think that I represented "professional and ethical sales and marketing" as the proper way to do business. I know you are of the same mind and focus.

There were many innovations that worked for me and many things that I tried that did not work. But I always tried to do things the right way and was rewarded in many ways for my efforts.

It is time for me to concentrate on other things now. The U.S. life expectancy is now 78.7 years and I still have energy to do my work in the death penalty abolition movement. The homicide rate in America is down to 4.7 per 100,000 adults, which is an improvement, but dismal when compared to Japan at 0.2, Germany 0.8, Australia 1.0, France 1.1, and Britain 1.2.

For a good number of years, I had my philosophy of life printed on my business cards: "Seek Peace, Give Service, Be Happy." I intend to continue living according to that philosophy. It is the core of my work and my life.

I am blessed to have a supportive and loving wife and family who allow me to pursue this work with gusto. I am ever mindful that I must also pay attention and provide time for them as well. So, between my desire to be the loving husband, father, and grandfather that I want to be, and to devote time to my peace-seeking life of service, I have come to this official life phase-change.

Gary, I know you will understand. I leave this phase of my life behind, knowing that you will uphold the principles of what I believed in, and worked so hard to instill in others, during my 47 years in the television business. It has been a great ride.

Peace,

Writing Your Own Obituary

A quick story here to explain why I've included my own obituary in these pages.

When Swedish chemist and inventor Alfred Nobel read his own obit in the newspaper one morning, he was aghast. It was published in error by an editor who mistook which Nobel brother had just died.

Alfred's discovery of dynamite had made him unimaginably wealthy, but he hated knowing that his legacy would mark him as "the man who made it possible to kill more people more quickly than anyone else who had ever lived." Soon thereafter, his will was changed, and the bulk of his estate was earmarked for establishing the Nobel Prizes, awarded annually for excellence in science, chemistry, medicine, literature, and peace.

So, each new class of students I taught at the Broadcast Sales Academy were encouraged to write their own obituary. I said to them, "When writing how you want to be remembered, you will undoubtedly mention something about the things you most value in life." When that was done, I would add, "Knowing what you've written about your life and the things you are proudest of, it's more likely that you will actually do those things, that you will live a life that honors the values you hold most dearly."

Obituary

Salem resident Ron Steiner passed away (date and place TBA). An Oregon resident since 2010, Ron moved here to live with his dear friend and wife, Caren Ann Jackson. He had previously lived in Albuquerque, New Mexico, for 30 years, where he rose to the top of his career and began to merge that life with one as a volunteer in service to a number of local, regional and national causes.

Ron was born on April 14, 1939, in Indiana, Pennsylvania and graduated from Allegheny College. He lived and worked in Pittsburgh for many years as an advertising salesperson and sales manager at the NBC network TV station. He moved to Albuquerque in 1980 to become the general manager at KLKK-TV, the state's first independent TV station. Because of his sales and leadership skills, the obscure station became financially successful and competitive in the Albuquerque market, with a small, creative staff. But then, with interest rates soaring to more than 20% during that time, the station owner replaced Steiner and eventually sold the station to a consortium headed by Johnny Carson and including Neil Simon, David Letterman, Joan Rivers, and Paul Anka.

"It turned out to be the best favor possible to me," said Ron, soon after being fired, as it led to the creation of the Marketing Communications Group, established to serve owners of other television stations with sales training, marketing, and management needs. He began with a small handful of TV stations but, over the years, Ron represented more than 150 stations nationwide as clients.

While managing that, he established a comprehensive sales curriculum which soon caught the attention of national media moguls and became the nucleus of the Broadcast Sales Academy, based in Dallas and serving major station-owner groups including Hearst, Belo, and Lin Broadcasting, with more than 100 TV stations between them nationally.

Toward the end of his professional career, Ron began applying his time, attention, energy, and marketing experience as a volunteer in New Mexico. He served as a volunteer and board member of Albuquerque Habitat for Humanity, Futures for Children, and Dismas House (a halfway house for formerly incarcerated men and women). Later, Ron served as a member of the Steering Committee for the New Mexico Coalition to Abolish the Death Penalty (which ultimately attained its goal in 2009), on the national board of directors for Murder Victims' Families for Reconciliation and as founder and Managing Director of the Albuquerque Italian Film Festival, a benefit for the New Mexico Children's Hospital.

After moving to Oregon, Ron continued his volunteer work as board chair of Oregonians for Alternatives to the Death Penalty until 2019.

He is survived by his son, Michael Ulku-Steiner, his wife Beril, and grandchildren Kenan and Lucy (Chapel Hill, NC); by his daughter Amy Halloran-Steiner, her husband Silas, and grandchildren Ukiah and Metolius (McMinnville) and by his wife Caren Ann Jackson, of Salem. Ron also has much-loved stepchildren and grandchildren in Oregon, Idaho, Washington, and Hawaii. Included are: Kari Lynn Kendall and husband Rick, and three grandchildren; Michael Mason and wife Cheryl, two grandchildren, and one greatchild; Gretchen Hollett and husband John, and two grandchildren; and Ryan Braunschweig.

Both Michael and Amy graduated from Albuquerque Academy, where they were high-achieving students and multiple letter-winners in sports. During the kids' pre-teen years, Ron served as coach for little league baseball, softball, and basketball teams in Albuquerque.

In Albuquerque, Ron was a member of Prince of Peace Catholic Community. In Salem, he and Caren Ann attended Queen of Peace Catholic church. His ashes will be scattered in Albuquerque, on the west face of the beautiful Sandia Peak.

Here are two of the posters for the Albuquerque Italian Film Festival, conceived by Ron in the early 2000s. He organized and ran the festival for five years, during which time the festival raised over $100,000 for the Univ. of New Mexico Children's Hospital.

seek PEACE.

seek PEACE.
give SERVICE.
be HAPPY.

PEACE

At some point in the late 1980s, in the pews of Prince of Peace parish church in Albuquerque, I was awake enough to hear Father Antonio Mondragon give a homily on forgiveness. Father Tony, as he was affectionately called, became my spiritual advisor. I learned many lessons from him by the way he related to the people in the pews, urging us to consider our relationship with God. Irreverent but always pious, Father Tony could make people understand when the facts or circumstances did not exactly square with the way we learned the differences between right and wrong.

On this occasion, Father Tony explained that forgiveness was more about the forgiver than the offender. The lesson was that when one was offended, or thought to be offended, the tonic for recovery was to forgive. Failing to forgive someone for an offense was allowing the offender to live rent-free in your mind.

The underlying lesson was that granting forgiveness provides peace of mind. Peace of mind is a mental state of calmness or tranquility, a freedom from worry and anxiety. Soon after, as I tried to make Father Tony's lesson a practice in life, I started to use "Peace" as a sign-off on all my correspondence. If the reader takes the use of "peace" as meaning "without war," that's OK by me, but as "peace of mind," it is meant to be more comprehensive, and more personal, in meaning.

The Inspiring Father Tony

Father Tony's tenure at Prince of Peace began sometime around 1984. Bishop Robert Sanchez sent him to serve as a temporary pastor of this new satellite church, funded by the Risen Savior Catholic community on Wyoming Blvd. in Albuquerque. Risen Savior's pastor was Father Paul Baca.

Prince of Peace was established to serve the fast-growing suburbs of Albuquerque Acres, Sandia Heights, and the High Desert community. Father Baca was known as a good money manager and steward of the church's treasures. Risen Savior owned property near Tramway Boulevard, designated for a future church. A residence and garage on the property was surrounded by enough acreage for a large church and plenty of parking. The parish community, just starting to grow, was too small to start building the physical structure, so the two-car garage was converted to accommodate meetings and weekend masses. We faithful parishioners called the building "Our Lady of the Garage."

Father Tony first served as an assistant at Risen Savior. Right away we lovingly embraced him as "our priest." One Sunday, a parishioner announced that Fr. Tony would not be available to say Mass due to a death in his family.

The next Sunday, when Fr. Tony returned to say Sunday mass, he started his homily with, "I have a confession to tell you. I was not totally honest that I was unavailable due to a death in my family. You need to know more. The death in my family was my daughter, who died in a car accident." The air filled with gasps from the 60 people in Our Lady of the Garage. First, we were gasping at the news of the young woman's death, and second, we were gasping that our priest had a daughter. Catholic priests do not, under normal circumstances, have children.

Father Tony continued, his parishioners hearing his confession. "When I was a young priest, I had a drinking problem and so I left the priesthood and got married. My wife and I had two children, a boy and a girl. It was my daughter we lost two weeks ago."

We listened intently.

"What you need to know is eventually my wife and I divorced, I got sober and tried to build my life back to a point where I could love myself, my church, and the people I could serve. Father Baca, who is my cousin, took me in to serve in any way that I could as a lay person."

A few years before coming back to New Mexico, Fr. Tony taught philosophy at UC Berkeley, one of the most prestigious universities in North America. We did not yet know much about this brilliant man, but we were fast appreciating his wisdom and experience.

The lay Antonio Mondragon did such a sterling job in service to the Risen Savior community and the church that Father Baca and the Archbishop of Santa Fe, Robert Sanchez, went to Rome to petition Pope John Paul VI to reinstate Antonio, former priest, married man, father of two children, recovering alcoholic and college professor, back into the priesthood and into service to Our Lady of The Garage.

That man and priest was so inspiring, the congregation grew swiftly. Everyone loved and admired our priest as fully as any clergy could be loved. Father Mondragon's love of God and willingness to serve allowed us to forgive him and be blessed by him.

My relationship with Father Tony included his help and support as I went through my own divorce in 1993. His example helped save my connection to the Catholic church and embodied the lessons of Jesus in a most human way.

The Perfect Life

What is your idea of perfect happiness?

My flippant reply to that question: a large bowl of ice cream every night before bedtime. That was possible at times in my life, but not anymore.

My honest answer is peace.

In my correspondence you may notice that I usually end with "peace." That could be a wish for peace in our relationship, in all our personal relationships, in our communities, and in the world in which we live.

My use of peace is intended as "peace of mind." This meaning encompasses all the above. Most of all, it describes a calm mind and loving heart.

What It Means to Seek Peace

My understanding of peace began as the fruit of forgiveness. As I continued to explore what peace of mind really means, I learned that living peacefully is a process rather than a request.

Here's how my friend, Gary Weber, put it so well in a short prose poem called, *We Are Here.*

"Instead of saying, 'I pray for peace,' say 'I intend peace, I am peace, I am the peace process!' And 'what I do becomes peace.' Thus, you can avoid attachment and acquisition. You do not seek to acquire peace or possess peace. You become peace."

When I end a letter, memo or email message, the valediction I use is Peace. The peace I wish for is peace of mind, a mind free of worry, of torment or of concern. Peace for the world is too big for me to suggest, but peace of mind is simple, personal, and totally accomplished if you are mindful. I am not suggesting, like Gary does (above) that you should seek peace as in prayer; rather, my suggestion is that you seek peace as a process achieved by being peaceful, mindful, and living well.

Thanks to Gary's words, my valediction can be better used and understood by me and by the people to whom I write.

It's Hard to Explain

The concept of peace can often take on spiritual meaning. This can be hard to explain, but I'll give it a try.

There is so much that we don't know. I don't mean the vast amount of information that we have not yet learned. Rather, I refer to all the things we cannot know - the "unknown."

Information increases exponentially, yet some thoughts and beliefs are beyond facts and proof. God, heaven, hell, the transfiguration of ordinary bread and wine into the body and blood of Christ, and the existence of the soul are a few concepts that billions of people believe are real, yet those concepts fall short of absolute knowledge. They cannot be proven.

The unknown is a mystery, unexplainable, so secret and obscure that it elicits everlasting curiosity. Mystery has always played a significant role in storytelling, literature, and history. The myths of ancient Greece, the Bible, and nursery rhymes are replete with tales that cannot be proven. Yet those stories persist.

Often explained and never proven, mystery adds palpable texture to our consciousness and to our unconscious dream world. Newton provided proof and explanation of the mystery of gravity. Columbus provided certainty and evidence that the world is round. Marconi explained the capacity of airborne electrons to carry sound and images. These are solved mysteries, revealed through inquiry, discovery, and inventions. So much is still unknown, but important to our existence. The mystery of the unknown excites us in a peculiar and compelling fashion.

Faith is the fruit of mystery. Without mystery – with complete certainty – there would be no need for faith. Faith supports us in the face of the unknown. It holds us fast when reason, logic and evidence are unavailable. It lifts us to personal enlightenment from the darkness.

Spirituality is the fruit of faith. To believe without proof, to gain understanding without evidence, to trust without tangible support, these all provide a coalescence of thought and feeling. Our spiritual self is not corporeal. It is a refinement of our intellect, driven and inspired by the ascendancy of heartfelt emotion. Spirituality opens us to deeper knowing, fuller understanding, greater emotion, and moral moments when we can see the world and each other with unqualified love. Spirituality is our connection to the entire universe and the admiration of its glory.

Soul is the fruit of the trinity of mystery, faith, and spirituality. Our soul is the immortal part of us, without physical properties. It manifests our moral and emotional natures. Our soul unseen reveals itself as love - love for ourselves, love for those with whom we share this universe, and love for the universe itself.

Do our souls live on after we die?
It is an unknown.
It is a mystery.
Have faith.
Enjoy the experience of it all.

Mystery, faith, and spirituality power our souls. They push us toward peace and happiness. So yes, I conclude that faith is not only peaceful, but it can be a path to happiness, too.

Enjoy the experience of it all.
Seek peace.
Be happy.

"Shit Happens"

Apologizing is often referred to as "asking for forgiveness." This essay was part of our training for TV advertising salespeople. It could work for any situation.

Even when our intentions are otherwise, things sometimes go wrong. Whenever this happens, here are some helpful and productive bits of advice I learned from author Ken Blanchard (in quotes, below). The way you handle the apology can help build a relationship to a point even higher than before the incident.

> *"The toughest part of apologizing is realizing and admitting that you were wrong. When things go wrong, one needs to stop phrases like 'should have, would have, and if.'"*

We judge ourselves by our intentions, while others judge us by our actions."

As soon as one realizes that they made a mistake, they need to quickly speak the truth and apologize. Mistakes left unattended can fester and poison relationships. "The weakness of failing to act promptly, honestly and openly can be perceived as wickedness by others, particularly the offended party."

Why do people not want to face the truth? "Because they don't realize that it's the truth that will set them free. The truth is intolerant of deception. There is either a right or wrong. The truth doesn't give people a lot of 'wiggle' room and, for some, that can feel very uncomfortable, especially living in a lie."

Blanchard was one of my best teachers. In his book, *The One Minute Apology,* he says an effective apology "begins with surrender and ends with integrity." The following portion is also from *The One Minute Apology:*

- "Recognize that what you did, or failed to do, is wrong and is inconsistent with who you want to be.

- Reaffirm that you are better than your poor behavior and forgive yourself.

- Recognize how much you have hurt others and make amends for the harm you caused.

- Make a commitment to yourself and others not to repeat the act and demonstrate your commitment by changing your behavior. Be specific and tell the people harmed exactly what you're apologizing for.

- After you tell someone specifically what you did wrong, the next step is sharing how you feel about what you did. Your feelings are strong enough that you want to change your behavior. By doing so you make the apology real and demonstrate your sincerity."

When it comes to customer service, as a salesperson or as one representing a non-profit organization, examine the options on how to make amends. Consider asking the offended:

- "How would you like to see the problem resolved?"

- "What would be an acceptable resolution for you?"

- "If you were in my position, how might you resolve this for your customer (or donor)?"

Many times, the offended customer or non-profit supporter will suggest something less onerous than what the offender was ready to offer. There are many examples and lots of evidence that when "shit happens" and the offender responds quickly, honestly, and with the assurance that they will try their best to avoid future problems, the relationship is strengthened. At some level, we all know that we are human, make errors and recognize our own failings in the behavior of the offender. There is a saying that goes something like, "It's not that you fell down, it is how well you got back up." The offended is likely to make mistakes, too, and they want to be forgiven when they get back up.

Forgiving oneself is also a very important thing. It is hard to apologize to others if we do not forgive ourselves first. We are human. We do make mistakes. We can learn from those mistakes and move on to do the right thing.

As Soon as You Think You Have It, It's Gone

At first, humility might seem like a necessary component to peace of mind, but it is more complicated than that.

It is like your lap: when you stand up, you lose it.

Humility, in various interpretations, is widely seen as a virtue that centers on low self-preoccupation, or unwillingness to glorify oneself. Humility is central in many religious and philosophical traditions.

One afternoon in the synagogue, a rabbi was overcome with rapture and threw himself to the ground proclaiming, "Lord, I am nothing!" Not to be bested, the cantor prostrated himself and exclaimed, "Lord, I am nothing!" The temple handyman, working in the back of the sanctuary, joined the fervor, prostrating himself and crying, "Lord, I am nothing!" Whereupon the rabbi nudged the cantor and whispered, "Look who thinks he's nothing!"

This joke captures what is frustrating about humility. Our attempts to be humble can easily backfire. Our wishes to be humble may be motivated by a deeper desire to be better than others. Our display of humility can be an occasion of pride. But how can we become humble if not by desiring humility and acting humbly? Maybe the pursuit of genuine humility is a fool's errand?

The Scottish philosopher David Hume thought so. He was suspicious of humility, along with many other virtues that Christians like to herald. He called them "monkish virtues." Hume claimed that although we appreciate displays of modesty, we do not genuinely value humility that "goes beyond the outside."

Who wants to hang around someone who really thinks they're nothing? Who wants to hire such a person?

What we appreciate, Hume suggested, is someone who is outwardly modest, but inwardly self-assured and motivated. That kind of person makes for an interesting friend and a valuable member of society. So don't waste your time trying to become genuinely humble. In the unlikely event that you succeed, you'll make yourself useless. Humility, Hume said, is really a vice.

We modern humans are inheritors of both the Christian promotion and Hume's Enlightenment-era criticism of humility. That's partly why we're so confused about humility—about what it is and whether we should want it. Most Americans, for example, would list humility as a virtue instead of a vice.

So, we are confused. We think humility will make us better people, which is another way of saying we think humility is a virtue. But we worry, along with Hume, that humility will prevent us from flourishing, which is another way of saying we worry that humility is a vice.

Before you decide whether it is a virtue or a vice, humility is worth more of your attention. Here are six habits that can help:

1. Spend time listening to others.
2. Practice mindfulness and focus on the present.
3. Be grateful for what you have.
4. Ask for help when you need it.
5. Seek feedback from others on a regular basis.
6. Review your actions against the language of pride.

seek PEACE.
give SERVICE.
be HAPPY.

give SERVICE.

seek PEACE.
give SERVICE.
be HAPPY.

MY LONGEST PROJECT

On May 1st of 2000, I heard Sister Helen Prejean speak at a fundraiser for the Albuquerque Dismas House. Dismas House, named after the "penitent thief" crucified on a cross adjacent to Jesus, is a place of transition and programming for formerly incarcerated felons rejoining society. Having begun as a volunteer cook and conversation partner once a week, I was then asked to serve on the Dismas House board of directors. I was also on the committee hosting the event.

Sister Helen spoke on her favorite theme: abolition of the death penalty.

She posed this question: "What percentage of the people in America who are tried, convicted and sentenced for capital murder get a death sentence?"

The answer: "Less than two percent. They are all poor and most of them are people of color," she said.

Having spent the first 60 years of my life thinking that the death penalty was a just sanction for the murder of another human being, I was shocked by her statement. The shock flipped a switch in my mind.

"That is simply not fair," I said aloud.

My belief in fairness took over and propelled me into motion. I committed to learn as much as possible about the American death penalty and the American criminal justice system.

The day after Sister Helen's speech was the beginning of my longest project. It continues because the mission is to abolish the death penalty in all of America. In New Mexico, we were successful in a state repeal in March 2009. I have since been focused on Oregon, where we celebrated the passage of Oregon Senate Bill 1013. The governor signed that bill into law on August 1, 2019.

Senate Bill 1013 reduces the number of aggravating factors that qualify a defendant to receive the death penalty, from nineteen to four. Experts note that the change will reduce the number of death cases in Oregon from 20 per year to two per year. The change in law makes it much more difficult to sentence someone to death in Oregon.

The project goes on. I am not deterred nor dispirited. I remain committed to finishing this project.

We still have another hurdle in Oregon, to remove the death penalty language from the state's Constitution. There are, additionally, many more death penalty hurdles nationwide, although to date, 23 states either prohibit the death penalty or have, like Oregon, put a moratorium on its practice, per the Governor's order.

Dear Governor Kitzhaber,

I have been in Oregon only about 12 years. You have been my governor and will always be my governor. You have seen my name come across your desk regarding our work on repeal of the death penalty.

I praise you for your courageous act of declaring the moratorium on executions and I will forever regard you as a hero for that act. Beyond that, I am proud to be an Oregonian and proud of the state where you have devoted so much time, energy, wisdom, and service. Oregon is what it is, in great part, for what you have contributed to it.

I am greatly saddened by the recent turn of events that led you to resign. These events, and your resignation, do not dim the esteem that I hold for you.

My best wishes for you continuing the work that you pledged to do in your resignation announcement. May you have good health, good friends, good support, and abundant love in your life as you carry on.

At the same time, I will carry on my efforts to repeal the Oregon death penalty. As a state, we can do better.

Peace,

Enlightened Inertia

Aristotle and the boys were sitting around in their togas, chins in hands, elbows on knees, contemplating why a stone hurled by a sling shot, much like the one David used to slay Goliath, sailed through the air as it did. Aristotle's account of motion was that a body only remained in motion by the action of a continuous external force. In his view, a projectile moving through the air would owe its continuing motion to eddies and vibrations in the surrounding medium.

This concept of things in motion has made me think about how people get into motion and do good work, such as activism on social justice issues. How does the discussion of physical properties of objects in motion relate to the emotional properties and actions of individuals?

It took several hundred years before Joannes Philoponus, during the sixth century, had the audacity to question the wisdom of Aristotle. Philoponus declared that motion was maintained by some property of the body, imparted when it was set in motion. The stone itself had an energy that was released when thrown. Roger Clemens' fastball was not Roger's doing, but rather the work of the rawhide orb itself. Aristotle's disciples went nuts at this suggestion.

Fast-forward another eight centuries, when Jean Buridan named the motion-maintaining property "impetus" and rejected the view that it dissipated spontaneously, asserting "that a body would be arrested by the forces of air resistance and gravity."

By the time that Isaac Newton finally got around to stating his *Law of Motion*, there had been considerable discussion about moving things. He declared:

"An object at rest tends to stay at rest and an object in motion tends to stay in motion with the same speed and in the same direction unless acted upon by an unbalanced force."

So here is this guy Newton, who is not even an elected official, making laws. Simply put, he says that objects keep doing what they're doing.

So, if Newton, who was not elected to any office, can make laws, I, who have never been elected to any office either, can take liberties

43

and use his law to make some points. My first is to state (this would be Ron's Law of Inactivity): people are like objects.

People have some of the same qualities as a stone, a baseball, a cow chip, or an orbiting planet. Some are at rest, and some are in motion. People tend to do the same things over and over, or refrain from doing anything at all.

I eat cottage cheese every morning, with fruit and nuts on it. I could eat eggs, or cereal, or donuts, but I keep doing the same thing, day after day. I originally had a reason to go on the aforementioned CCF&N breakfast diet, but now I don't remember why. Yet, I still do it. Some people vote Republican, because they always have (and their parents did before them), without knowing exactly why, without knowing what the Republican political philosophy stands for, and without researching the character of the ones wearing the elephant buttons. (You can easily interchange Democrats and donkey buttons for the above). Some people have cable television in their homes, with its 80 different channels. The average American household could look at 80 different channels, but they really only look at about 12 of those offered. They keep paying ever-increasing rates without an analysis of their expenditures and how cable television enhances or diminishes their lives.

Inertia affects people to a very great degree. We keep doing what we have been doing, in the absence of (as Newton stated) "an unbalanced force" or what Galileo called "forces impressed on it." So, what does it take? What does it take to get people to stop what they are doing or to get them into motion? What does it take to get someone to stop smoking, when their entire rational being knows that smoking is not good for them? What does it take for a person to leave an abusive relationship? What are the "unbalanced forces" that cause us to form a committee and fight crime in our neighborhoods? What are the "forces impressed on us" that make us change our positions on a social, political or justice issue that we cling to as tightly as the lid on a pickle jar?

From the age of reason, until just past my 60th birthday, I believed that very bad people, people who killed another human being, deserved the death penalty. In my mind, that was justice. Do something terrible, something terrible should happen to you.

Soon after that 60th birthday, I heard a speech by Sister Helen Prejean, the author of Dead Man Walking. She was speaking at a fund-raiser for a transition program for ex-offenders where I was a volunteer. Sister Helen's remarks included some of her experiences working with death row inmates and with murder victims' families.

I was astonished to learn that less than two percent of people convicted of a capital crime get a sentence of death. The unassuming nun cited figures showing that those few who did get death sentences were overwhelmingly poor, people of color and inadequately represented at trial by court-appointed attorneys. Sister Helen colorfully proclaimed, "There are the O.J.s and the No J's."

This was the first "force impressed" on my mind at rest. I had been content with my uninformed position on the death penalty. It dawned on me, "That isn't fair."

She went on. Since the Federal death penalty was re-instated in 1976 there have been an increasing number of death sentences overturned by post-trial investigation, new DNA evidence and confessions by the real killers. There are mistakes by our system of justice. Mistakes made by judges who provided wrong instructions to juries. Inept defense lawyers who were drunk or fell asleep during trial. Convictions made on the basis of witnesses who were guilty themselves and used the innocent to escape their own punishment. This new information was the "impressed force" for me.

This information shook me like an earthquake shakes the windows of buildings far from the epicenter. I was far from the courtrooms where justice was tainted. I was far from the reality of a life taken by error, inadequacy, or contempt. But I felt the shaking.

If over 100 convictions were overturned by mistakes, how many death row inmates were executed before the truth was known? "That isn't fair," yelled the voice in my head, a new "impressed force" ushered in with her new information.

Based on her work with victims' families, Sister Helen shared that while everyone wants justice, few members of victim's families find closure in the execution of yet another human being. "An eye for an eye" doesn't really work. The subsequent death of a convicted murderer never brought the victim back and seldom brings solace to family and loved ones.

The "force" now had me in motion. Sister Helen had ignited in me a torch that, when held high, provided illumination. I read her book. I read several other books on the death penalty. I read books about the Bible quotations that could support either side of the controversy. I read articles and listened to speeches. I started to create my own force by discussing the topic of the death penalty with anyone who was willing to encounter someone in motion. I continued to learn. I learned right away that many people, maybe most people, are like I was, uninformed yet holding onto a position. We were minds and emotions at rest.

After joining the ranks of death penalty abolitionists, I began encountering people who were very much in motion in a direction opposite of mine. When we met, it was like an immovable object and an irresistible force. Something ought to give, I thought, but my experience was different when it came to this particular social justice issue.

I really do not mind if I encounter a view contrary to mine, as long as the person has really been thinking about the subject and knows something about it. Knowledge is the "force." Information counters inertia. Thought is the torch that lights our way to a more civilized society. Like Aristotle, Philoponus, Buridan, da Vinci, Galileo, and Newton, we should all put our heads in our hands, our elbows on our knees and think about important aspects of us sharing this universe with others. Ask the "why" questions. Then, let's get off our asses and put something in motion. Resting or moving, enlightened activity is a very good thing.

(A letter to the Salem Statesman Journal about the death penalty)

Dear Capi,

Congratulations!

You did a wonderful, marvelous, and sensitive job in Sunday's feature about the murders of Karissa Fretwell and her son William. The way that you portrayed Karissa's mother and other family members was touching. Many times, you mentioned the wonderful work of law enforcement and the DA's office. You also pointed out the difficulties of such a terrible case.

I also appreciate the fact that you mentioned later in the article that the law in Oregon has changed, making it more difficult to seek a death penalty. That made it even more meaningful to read that Karissa's mom and other family members chose not to seek a death case, but one more fitting for her family, for the state of Oregon, and for many people in the DA's office.

Although the journey was long and difficult, a "death case" would have lingered on for many more years. Mr. Wolf, the convicted killer, most likely would not be executed. There would be no closure for the family and loved ones, and the DA's office would be required to labor on at the expense of other criminal justice activities in Yamhill County.

A confession and expected sentence of life in prison, with the possibility of parole only after Mr. Wolf's 85th birthday, makes more sense for everyone.

I have worked over 20 years to abolish the death penalty and six years on the national Board of Directors of Murder Victim Families for Reconciliation.

In my expansive work as a victims' advocate, I have encountered hundreds of families who made bad decisions by seeking death. I have seen many more positive decisions by families who sought an alternative. Revenge in the form of an execution never provides family members with an outcome that is satisfying. Remembering Karissa and William in a loving manner is far healthier than seeking an unfulfilling revenge.

Capi, the wonderful work you did telling the story is a blessing for the family and loved ones of Karissa and William, along with all of Yamhill County.

Peace,

Ron

PS: We should also offer our hearts and prayers to Mr. Wolf's family. They must deal with the shame and sorrow brought on by his senseless, terrible actions.

Additional Thoughts on the Tragedy of the Death Penalty

The following are quotes from Sister Helen Prejean about an Ohio execution, in December 2019:

> As together we say no to this state killing, we also hold central in our hearts Sheila Marie Evans. This little girl of three was raped, beaten, and murdered.

> Her killing was a terrible act. There is no shying away from that fact. We acknowledge it, we mourn her loss, and we recognize the terrible pain of her loss to her family.

> At the same time, we must oppose the state committing another terrible act, an execution, supposedly in the name of justice.

Brutality for brutality is not justice. It is barbaric revenge.

And there should be no doubt that an execution is a brutal, moral horror. We try our best to mask that, to sanitize the process, but it is an undeniably brutal act that brutalizes us as a society.

We shelter ourselves from this truth by hiding the execution away in a tiny chamber with only a few witnesses. Those witnesses are further protected from the truth because mixed into the lethal cocktail that is injected into the prisoner is a paralytic agent, whose sole purpose is to mask the suffering this human being is experiencing.

We must be brave enough to look squarely at both moral horrors: the death of a little girl on the one hand and the state-sanctioned murder of an adult man on the other. We must look at them both and then choose life. Choosing life for an innocent is an easy thing to do; choosing life for the guilty is a far harder thing. But it is what we must do *if we truly stand for life.*

Statement of Timothy F. Sweeney and Lisa M. Lagos, attorneys for Ronald Phillips, on his execution day for the murder of that little girl:

"We extend our heartfelt condolences to the Evans family for their loss. And to the Phillips family for theirs.

Ron Phillips committed an unspeakable crime when he was 19 years old and was himself the product of a home filled with abuse and neglect. But the grown man who woke up this morning at age 43, ready to face his punishment, did not in any way resemble that troubled and broken teen. He had grown to be a good man who was thoughtful, caring, compassionate, remorseful, and reflective. He tried every day to atone for his shameful role in Sheila's death. In the past years, Ron studied for and earned his certification to be a minister and was preparing his first sermon. It was entitled 'My People.'"

Just Visiting

The door slammed shut behind me. Its heavy thud was followed by a distinct metallic click. Not your normal household door. The weight of the door was ominous enough, but the click provided certainty. I was locked in.

The doors of prisons are different. They look different, sound different, feel different and serve a very different purpose. Most doors lock to keep the unwanted out. Prison doors lock, double lock, electronically lock, and slam shut locked, to keep the unwanted inside.

I had never been in a prison before. Now a powerful slamming sound assured me that I was inside a high-level security lockup. I was there to meet Dennis Harrison for the first time. A friend had asked me to write to him, because he had no family and no visitors. After a few letters, I knew that I must meet this man. This gentle, spiritual, articulate person was in the state's only maximum security prison, known as Oregon State Penitentiary, or OSP. Going there made me nervous. I was unsure of the procedures. The visitors' rules for OSP are many, including hours, dress code, possessions one can carry in, and identification.

I climbed the cold stone steps to the entry. There were two doors. The visitors' door required you to buzz in so that the guard on duty could release the heavy latches. Once inside, it was institutional looking. All gray. Gray, spit-shined floors, gray walls, a gray counter staffed by two guards in gray uniforms.

After checking in, I was politely asked to take a seat on one of the gray chairs in the waiting room. I was nervous, partly because of the jailhouse surroundings and partly because I was unsure about visiting this person who I only knew from a few letters.

I needed to sit while enough visitors assembled, so that guards could take a group of us to the actual visiting room. When there were about 15 people in the well-scrubbed foyer, we were all asked to go through a security check. Like an airport metal detector, we passed through one-by-one. As each person passed inspection, we were asked to again wait until everyone had passed the scrutiny of the electronic sensors. The group was then ushered by one guard in front, and another guard in back, through a doorway. This time a door of thick bars unlocked and then slid to the side electronically. Someone in a glass-enclosed room that resembled the director's booth in a TV station newsroom, with many monitors and panels of switches, was signaled by our following guard to close the bars behind us.

The group was led down a ramp. Once the trailing guard had passed through, the door behind us slid back into place and locked with a resounding clang. As we proceeded down the ramp, we were in a cell of our own, as we now faced yet another heavy metal sliding door. The lead guard signaled to the controller inside the booth and the door slid open. We proceeded down another hallway where we were told to walk single file against the left wall and stop at the doorway on the right.

A guard inside the visiting room peered out though a tiny double-glass window for the signal to open the door from the inside. Finally, we were ushered in. Once we were all in, the deafening SLAM of the door again reminded us of our inescapable situation.

Inside were facing rows of metal chairs with fake leather seat covers and backs. Visitors were to sit on the outside rows, inmates on the inside rows. Between us were small tables. The seats were close together, allowing no real privacy. Since weekly visiting hours are restricted and OSP houses over 2,000 inmates, the small visiting space was crowded. I had to remind myself that these men were in here because they were found guilty of crimes and were being punished. Why would I think it was the lobby of the Hilton?

I found a chair and waited for my first in-person connection with my pen pal. My visit with Dennis went well. Nervousness melted away immediately by his grateful and gracious nature. The conversation went deep; those seated close faded from vision and consciousness. We had several visits at OSP before he was transferred to Mill Creek Correctional Institution, an "honors" facility with less rigid security.

During every visit to the penitentiary, the visitor is seated before the inmate arrives. While waiting, sometimes it is hard not to look around, peering into intimate conversations that are going on between prisoners and their friends and loved ones. I always tried to be respectful and mannerly, yet full of curiosity about these people. What was their story? Why were they there? Were they bad people, or just people from bad circumstances or people who made bad choices? Who loves them? Visitors must love them because there is little that is pleasant about entering the grim prison environment. The whole ordeal reminds visitors and inmates alike that the "screws" are in control, totally in control.

Mill Creek houses people soon to be released. This smaller structure perches high on a hill overlooking lush farm fields east of Salem. The driveway is a short distance up a hill off the road to Turner, a suburb of Salem. The parking lot is only steps from a loading dock, with a VISITORS sign pointing to a door. Here, unlike the three-chambered ordeal of OSP, a guard came out the entry door and passed a metal-detecting wand over and around us. Then, we simply walked inside, signed in at the nearby desk, and we were right there in the visiting area. The space was really a cafeteria doubling as a visiting room. Visitors came to one end and found a seat at one of the four-place, round dining tables. I waited for my friend to appear.

Again, during the wait, my glances darted around the room, noticing the men, wondering about the visitors. As discretely as possible, I started to watch the way that visitors and inmates greeted. It was easy to spot parents of young inmates. Most hugged. Girlfriends and wives kissed their men, but always in an urgent manner. I later learned that there is a six-second time limit on kisses at the beginning and end of visits. Sometimes, what I imagined when a father greeted his son, offering only a handshake, was that maybe he was continuing to withhold affection. Did he love his son? What was their relationship while the inmate was growing up? Could the father not get over the embarrassment of having a convicted criminal for a son?

When my wait was longer, I would survey the population demographically, age groupings and ethnic mix. Most were young. A large percentage were men of color, in a predominantly white state. Are Blacks and Latinos more apt to be criminals? I know enough about crime and crime prevention to know that Blacks and Latinos are more apt to be poor. My guess is that most of these men were poor, had always been poor.

Since the seating was for four, and we were only two, sometimes we were asked to share the table with another inmate and his visitor. That discomfort again diminished as we fell into our own intimate conversation. I learned much about Dennis' past and more of his hopes for the future. This was the kind of stuff that I wondered about when watching others. So, I suppose all of them had stories to tell.

Dennis was at Mill Creek for only a short time. He told me that although OSP was at a much more heightened security level, living conditions were better there. Mill Creek was very overcrowded. Sleeping was dormitory-style and always noisy. No place to find any private time....no place to exercise....no place to engage in the Buddhist practices that had helped Dennis turn his life around. While the label was "lower security," the reality was "we are still in control."

From Mill Creek, Dennis was moved down the hill to Santiam Correctional Facility, another large facility within sight of the former lockup. Again, Santiam was different in its security configurations. It was still gray in color and dulling to the senses. Off the parking lot, with a view of the "yard" as well as the dormitory and administration buildings, was a guardhouse that provided entry. Individuals or groups entered the small space. Inside a glass cage, a guard signed you in and verified you from a computer list of registered visitors. Another guard "wanded" you before you could join a group being escorted up a covered sidewalk, in sight of the men exercising in the yard, into a receiving room.

You could imagine that the men on the inside were watching the visitors, longing for contact with someone who cared about them. "No visitor again today," I imagined I would say in their place, "I'll run some laps to work off my frustration and loneliness."

Once the group was assembled inside, we were led down a long corridor, over spotless gray floors, past several rooms and locked doorways to another cafeteria that served as the visiting room on weekends.

The tables here were like those at Mill Creek. Since this was a bigger facility, it was usually very crowded, always noisy and, in the summer, beastly hot. Cooling fans only added to the noise. Most times Dennis and I shared one of the round tables with another inmate and his visitor. Guards' eyes were ever-present. No talking to anyone at another table. No physical contact other than your greeting and goodbye. "We are watching you" was the constant message. My time spent waiting provided more time to continue my silent survey of others suffering the punishment of their sentence.

I noticed more evidence of varied stories. Some of the prisoners who sported the most tattoos had visitors who were equally adorned with body art. Some of the prisoners had so many tattoos that I could not tell where one started and another ended. Like graffiti on passing train cars, you could not read it and wondered why it was there in the first place.

I looked at the men and observed their visitors. Often, I would guess what their lives were like together before they were incarcerated. The number of visitors who went there and played cards with the inmate often surprised me. So little time together. Did they have so little to talk about that they passed their scarce time in silent shuffling, dealing, and laying down numbered icons of mystery?

Dennis finally got released from prison but by then I would visit another prisoner, named Noble, at nearby Oregon State Correctional Institution, known as OSCI. This is the fourth state facility I've encountered in Marion County, where there is a concentrated number of prisons and a state mental hospital. I call it criminal warehousing. At some point in the state's history someone determined prisons were a form of economic development and job creation. That's when they began to build prisons in other towns. Still, there are more than 4,000 people locked up in the immediate Salem area .

OSCI again has different security measures. As you move along the driveway, you pass under a guard tower. Here a sign signals you to stop and report your purpose into a faceless intercom. The voice, which comes from above, directs you where to park and when to proceed to the gatehouse. Like Santiam's gatehouse, one passes through the metal detector and registers with the gray-clad guard. I continue to be impressed that the guards, with few exceptions, have been business-like, with subdued cordiality. When one of them has an attitude, it is quite evident to me, just looking at their countenance and body language.

Once leaving the guardhouse, you proceed unattended along a sidewalk that passes a very well-equipped playground. I usually go to OSCI during the week and have yet to see children playing on the brightly painted swings, slides, and merry-go-round. Its horse, rhino, dolphin, and swan are a vivid contrast to the grayness of being inside.

OSCI's visiting room seems to be dedicated purely for visiting. Again, there are rows of chairs, with small tables between facing positions. The visitors sit in the blue outer row, while the inmates are to sit on the inner, orange-backed, seats. The closeness of the seats, even on less-crowded weekdays, provides the opportunity to eavesdrop and the distracting loss of privacy. It took more time for Noble to feel comfortable speaking deeply with me. Lately, that has become a reality and very satisfying. He has never seemed to mind being close to the others in the room.

When I thought about that, why should he? He lives this way 24/7. And, he has lived that way for more than a few years. He is used to this aspect of paying one's debt to society.

On one recent visit, while I waited, I was seated close to a young man and his female visitor. From the conversation, which I did not want to share but could not avoid, I could tell that the inmate had great anger. I could not imagine why the woman wanted to be there with him. His hostile tone was peppered with profanity, insults, and contemptuous words for her. He berated her for everything from her unavailability when he attempted to call, to whom she was spending time with while he was biding his time in one of Oregon's human warehouses, to how much weight she had gained. His nervous mannerisms suggested that he was still going through some sort of detox process. I reflected on how many others at OSCI were filled with that type of rage, and how many others Noble must live side-by-side with. I realized this was yet another depressing reality of the punishment.

Lately I have been noticing the inmates' hair. Everything from clean-shaven heads to locks below the shoulder. Many sported facial hair. Some were quite creative. Mustaches, goatees, full beards, long beards that are braided, sideburns of varying lengths, every imaginable style of haircut and facial hair. Noble wears his hair long, down to his shoulders, or braided in the back, with a well-trimmed goatee and mustache.

Why not do something with your hair? All the men wear the exact same denim blue uniforms, stenciled with INMATE, in orange paint. They all eat the same starchy food, in the same sanitized gray dining halls. They all sleep in same-sized cells, walk and exercise on the same schedule. They all interact with the gray guards. One of the few ways to distinguish oneself is how you wear your hair. A simple difference, but important. Knowing oneself must be hard in prison. The homogenized environment leaves little opportunity to create identity. Recognition must be one of the basic human needs, along with food, shelter, water, safety, love, human contact. Recognition means "I see you as a person, an individual."

I'm just visiting, getting to understand my friends on the inside, the subtleties of the punishment our society doles out, and my own attitudes toward those often considered as "un-wanted."

Dennis Harrison Eulogy

I first met Dennis in 2001, while he was doing time in the Oregon State Penitentiary (OSP). The meeting was suggested by Caren Ann and her best buddy, Lani O'Callahan. Lani met Dennis when conducting "shoulder to shoulder" discussion groups between outside volunteers and a similarly-sized assembly of willing inmates. Lani and Caren Ann thought Dennis would like to have a pen pal with someone beyond the walls of OSP.

Within a few letters, the relationship went from pen pal to visitor to a friendship to a solid relationship.

When we first met, Dennis had been in custody for 26 of his 52 years on this planet. I thought he must be a really bad dude. I was wrong.

Rather than tell everything here, I will jump to the end of his story, when I was honored and humbled to speak about him at his funeral. Here's what I said:

In this gathering is a great diversity of spiritual beliefs and faith traditions. While we may be different in how we observe, pray, ask for mercy, and share our rituals, we all have the commonality of being of gracious heart and having a loving connection to our brother Dennis Harrison. We are all here because we care about Dennis and about the tenderness that each of us has in our own way, stemming from our own individual experiences with Dennis. Since first learning the news of his death, I have certainly felt the comfort of this community sharing our grief. So many expressions of love, of gratefulness for having known this man, and of compassion for each other as we deal with our loss.

May my words reflect your feelings and fuel the warm flame of memory that each of you may have for Dennis.

Before I first met Dennis in person, I corresponded with him for several months when he was in OSP. Quickly, in spite of the most difficult handwriting I have ever read, I learned the depth of this man. He reinforced what I had learned several years earlier, while volunteering at a transition program in New Mexico, for former felons who were returning into the community. If we are all judged by our worst deeds and we judge others by their best deeds, we are all very close in moral fiber.

I quickly found Dennis to be a spiritual man who came from a place where one would not expect the depth of thought, the goodness, the understanding, the insight, and the compassion.

When I was then able to visit with Dennis, I grew in admiration and appreciation for him. We were able to have wonderful, deep discussions about concepts and philosophies that I rarely was able to share with others, particularly with male friends. Women recognize that most men would rather go to their caves to figure things out by themselves, quietly, alone, uninterrupted, without talking. The male process is different. Well, Dennis and I did talk out loud to each other. We processed what we felt and what we believed.

We shared how we got to our respective levels of understanding and knowing. Although we followed different paths to that knowing, we communed in many ways. One of the things that we shared was a belief that all emotions flow from a bi-modal core in us, made up of one part love and one part fear. If you can imagine something deep in our bellies that looks like a two-spouted jug, a two-module squash, or two fists woven together side by side. One is the life-spring of love, the other the headwaters of fear. Our emotions come from this epicenter that has been formed by all our experiences and our knowing. They are the lessons we have learned through our intuition.

This internal battery sends the electric charges that stimulate our emotions. Depending on the make-up of our own unique core, we act and react with different emotions. Those emotions come from one side or the other of our internal fountainhead, flowing from one of the two emotional nozzles.

From the love side comes kindness, gentleness, compassion, forgiveness, sweetness, caring, patience, calm, tenderness, and consideration.

From the fear side comes anger, hatred, rage, deceit, and destructive emotions that cause harm to us or to others.

When trying to understand ourselves, when we identify the source of our emotions, love, or fear, we are better able to understand them. We can recognize them and know what those emotions feel like and then do something with them. When we understand what those emotions are, and where they came from, then we can control them when they are harmful, and experience the ultimate joy of them when they are wholesome.

Another philosophy that we talked about was a concept that I learned from Dennis: ripples. Many of you have heard him talk about ripples, good and bad. The ripples emanate from our actions. Good ripples help others, make them feel good or make them better off. Bad ripples harm others, make them feel bad or make them worse off. The concept is so simple and at the same time so powerful. What is not so simple is the number of ripples that flow from our actions, good and bad, the distance that they travel, and the number of people that they can touch. Our actions are not confined to simplistic touching of just one person. When considered deeply, they can be recognized as ebbing on endlessly.

Another philosophy or concept that we talked about was that of scarcity and abundance. This also ties into the sources of our emotions and the ripples. When we think in terms of scarcity, we are dealing with fear. Not enough to eat. Not a big enough car. Not having the best seat in the theater. Scarcity may cause us not to share when we really could.

When we think in terms of abundance, we can afford to be generous, to share, to make sure that others are provided for. Some of the things that are unfathomably abundant are God's love, beauty, goodness, kindness, appreciation, a mother's love, colors of the fall, and stars in the sky. When we think in terms of abundance, we can afford to be creative enough to make sure that everyone gets what they want from a relationship, a conversation, a table of food. Abundance is relative and defined in one's own mind. Dennis understood these concepts. To a great degree he lived these philosophies and sometimes (like all of us) forgot the importance of them.

When Dennis died, my emotions ran high and my mind raced from one image to another, from one question to another, from one memory to another, from the impact that his passing had on me to the impact that his passing had on others. One of the thoughts that kept coming back into this cyclone of my mind was that I was happy for Dennis that he no longer needed to suffer the earthly pain that he had known.

Another recurring thought was the gladness that Dennis got to experience in the last years of his life that were new to him. He created rich, wonderful, and lasting memories for us here and for him in eternal life. Dennis got to know some things that only he could absorb in his soul. Dennis got to glow in the warmth of the real love of a wonderful woman. Dennis got to know the embrace of an entire community, even more than one community.

Dennis got to have the pride of creating good ripples by sharing the few earthly possessions he had with homeless people under the Marion Street Bridge. He recognized that those people had less.

Dennis got to feel the respect of people in various stations in this community. Those who knew Dennis understand how important having respect was to him. What he sometimes forgot, like many of us sometimes forget, is that respect must be earned. Dennis also got to feel the love provided by Rose and John (from the Church here), who treated him like a son.

For the first time in his life, Dennis got to know the happiness of holding a newborn, my granddaughter Ukiah, closing his eyes and feeling the warm tears of pure joy run down his cheek.

Dennis got to experience the importance of creating favorable ripples and then seeing the gratitude flow back when he would help Nancy Morley with her yard work, or be in communication with his young friend David on the east coast, or help a friend in prison endure the hardships of confinement, or lend his pickup to someone who needed to carry a heavy load. Dennis was a part of the reciprocity of life, where goodness, kindness and favors are a currency. He was able to make many deposits and enjoy the fruits of many withdrawals. We need to keep in mind that the only currencies that really matter in life are peace and love.

Dennis got to tend to Mother Earth with great skill and caring. The Hope Plants that are scattered around our community are examples of how close he felt to nature.

Dennis got to go back to his mother and reunite in the most loving, joyful, and everlasting ways. These and many other things Dennis got to know, despite the many years when it seemed he would never have those opportunities.

Dennis did get to live the richness of having people who knew, respected, loved, and appreciated him. Some of us are right here in this holy place. Being here to remember Dennis makes it holy. Being connected to Dennis, for as long as we had him, helped to make him whole.

May the long time sun shine upon you all love surround you. May the pure light within you guide your way on.

How Our Country Has Changed

When I reflect on the positive and negative changes I have seen in my lifetime, I believe that service might be as important for us collectively as individually.

Much has changed in my lifetime. Some of the changes have been good and others have diminished the luster of America. Since my birth year, in 1939, the country has endured multiple military conflicts: WWII, Korea, Vietnam and, more recently, wars in Kuwait, Iraq, and Afghanistan.

Countless and horrific numbers of those fighting have died, been wounded, or suffered PTSD. To some degree or another, all who survived have suffered "moral wounds." Except for WWII, the conflicts were for the wrong reasons - to maintain "American interests." In my view, American interests were selfish, greedy, and false positions pushed by the military-industrial complex.

The government should never lie to its citizens. In much of my lifetime, the government has lied. Presidents Johnson and Nixon lied. Defense Secretary McNamara lied, prolonging the Vietnam War. Those lies set up a situation that turned much of the country against the noble soldiers who went there not knowing the evil nature of those leaders.

A more complex and ambiguous change: the American interstate highway system. From the day President Dwight D. Eisenhower signed the Federal-Aid Highway Act of 1956, the interstate system has been a part of our culture - as massive construction projects, as smooth transportation in our daily lives, and as an integral part of the American way of life.

The American interstate highway system dramatically and swiftly changed our country from an urban and rural culture to an urban, suburban, and rural culture. With speedy highways, there was a need for more automobiles, new types of housing, shopping centers and going cross county, rather than down the block to visit relatives and friends. The highway system fostered growth in many industries and turned us into the biggest energy-guzzling nation in the world.

The early years created growth, progress, and culture. Now we are learning the negative impact of excessive use of carbon-based energy products. It is important that we make the quick and proper decisions to change policy to save the environment and the health of the Earth.

I could offer many more changes but will just comment on one. From the end of WWII until the 1970's, the capitalistic policies that were enacted fueled the best economy in the world. Gradually, but clearly in the 70's, government policies began to change.

The exceptionalism that most Americans believed to be true started to slowly fade. The attitude was focused on "personal responsibility." For those less blessed, they were told that their success hinged solely on their own choices and actions. "Pull yourself up by your bootstraps" (a funny thing to say when we think about how difficult that action really would be!) From the Reagan administration forward, government policies, tax laws and federal programs to help people succeed have all withered.

In the early days, particularly in the West, this country was developed with a "homestead" policy where people were given plots of land and stipends to get started. This was pure and simple "socialism."

Another "help all" government policy was the development of the state college/university systems. Following WWII, returning military vets were helped by the GI Bill, allowing college education or trade education - another socialistic policy that has over time diminished. Today, millions of hard-working men and women find themselves paralyzed by student loans after striving their way through college and graduate schools. For this and other reasons, they cannot afford the kinds of homes that were so abundantly affordable to their parents and grandparents.

Our country was also built on the United States Social Security program (FDR in 1935) and 30 years later, Medicare and Medicaid (1965). While not called "socialist" programs, they certainly provided all citizens degrees of security. "All citizens" was a key aspect of these programs.

The policies changed to the disadvantage of public education, health care policy and programs to afford some degree of security. When emphasis swung to "personal responsibility," the government and tax code began to favor those blessed with more over those having less. These policies were never stated as racist, but certainly did not favor non-white Americans.

The Civil Rights Movement of the 1960's raised fears among the white privileged leaders and policymakers that everything they had could be at risk. Subtly, but surely, things started to change. Simmering below the surface was the racist, slave holder history that is with us still.

Beyond the population growth of African Americans in the U.S., the numbers of Latinos, Asians and Pacific Islanders started to grow. People of color struggled to achieve equal rights and equal opportunities. They, along with those disabled, continued to be marginalized in the "land of the free" by economic, social, and political realities that favored white, able-bodied, and already privileged Americans.

Despite the imbalance in treatment, those in power and the media continued to pump sunshine up the ass of much of the country, that America was "special" and "#1 In the World." As time passed, world surveys and world organizations revealed the truth that (again) the nation was being lied to. "American exceptionalism" is fake news.

Some recent studies point out that the U.S. is lagging behind other modernized countries. The 2019 Bloomberg Study has us ranked at #36 with a Health Rating of 73.83, while the top three (Spain, Italy, and Iceland) are all well above 90.

While our neighbor to the north gets berated for its socialized health care system, Canada has a life expectancy of 82.2 compared to our 79.3. In infant mortality, Canada is at 4.9 per 1,000 live births, compared to the U.S. rate of 6.5. All the while, the U.S. per capita annual health care expenditure is $9,403 and Canada is $5,292. Instead of making progress, we are falling behind.

Wake up America. Get off your over-weight ass, learn the facts. Change the government leaders and the policies that are driving us toward the bottom.

This I Believe: Time For Another "Cold War"

Following World War II, the Western democracies and the Soviet Union, former allies against Nazi Germany, entered a period of history that we commonly refer to as The Cold War. A cold war is one in which opposite sides pose and rattle their sabers, yet stop short of actual conflict with each other. A cold war differs from a hot war, when actual fighting results in destruction, death, and devastation upon the warring parties. A cold war is a standoff of sorts. Standoffs occur when bullies of equal strength flex their muscles yet remain frozen in fear of the opponent's fighting forces.

The Cold War started with post-war discussions in 1943. At that time, it was a political conflict between the members of NATO (North Atlantic Treaty Organization) and the nations of the Warsaw Pact. It was also a difference in economic ideology between capitalism and socialism, the free world versus communist totalitarianism. It was often viewed as East versus West, separated by what Winston Churchill dubbed the "Iron Curtain." The Iron Curtain was an imaginary border between the European nations of the West and those of the Warsaw Pact.

The United States was the lead country of NATO and was known as a "superpower." The Soviet Union was also a superpower, distinguished in an equally ominous manner. From the late 1940's until the breakup of the Soviet Union in 1991, the superpowers never went to war with each other. A war between them could have signaled the end of the world.

Imagining the end of the world was possible, due to the many technological advances in military armament and general science. During this period, the USA and the Soviet Union were in an arms race that included the development of jet fighters, bombers, nuclear weapons, chemical weapons, biological weapons, surface-to-air missiles, surface-to-surface missiles, inter-continental ballistic missiles, anti-ballistic missile technology, spy satellites and a growing mass of menacing machines and methodologies.

Through the years it was:

Truman *vs.* Stalin
Eisenhower *vs.* Khrushchev
Kennedy *vs.* Khrushchev
Johnson *vs.* Kosygin
Nixon/Ford *vs.* Brezhnev
Reagan *vs.* Gorbachev

They stared each other down but kept their guns in their holsters.

When the Berlin Wall was finally torn down and the Soviet Union collapsed, the world was left with one superpower, the United States of America, the One World Bully.

Under the leadership of a vengeful, imperialistic, and swaggering George W. Bush, the United States wielded too much power. President Bush was able to convince most of our Washington lawmakers, and much of the constituency of this country, that certain countries threaten our supremacy by their own development and possession of "weapons of mass destruction." Without proving his premise, he ordered an invasion of Iraq, spent billions upon billions of the country's resources, and placed American men and women in harm's way. This was a hot war, to be sure, with a high count of American injured and dead. There were also countless numbers of Iraqi casualities, many of them innocent people, women, children, the elderly.

Why? To "rid the world of terrorists." To "create democracies." To "remove brutal dictators." To "advance the interests of the United States."

The "interests of the United States" is Bush-speak for the interests of the United States' military-industrial establishment. The General Electrics, the Bechtel's, the Halliburton's, the Lockheed Martins of this great nation, and the oil companies . . . oh yes, the oil companies. These companies were all strong supporters of Mr. Bush.

So now the emerging threat to the supremacy of the world's one superpower is Iran. Known and admitted to having a program to develop weapons of mass destruction, Iran looms as a country that could also rattle a nuclear sword.

Since the United States has the greatest stockpile of weapons of mass destruction and, under Bush, was led by a fundamentalist Christian—someone who I suspect of irrational thinking and behavior,—why not have another country, a country populated by fundamentalist Muslims, led by someone who talks like he is very rational, possess a somewhat equal threat? Maybe there could be another Cold War. It could be one where we did not actually go to war, where the "leaders" just rattled their swords and let people live.

Having just seen three films by Iranian directors and about Iranian people, I have a renewed belief that the people of Iran are no more evil than the people of the United States. They are religious people. They are God-fearing people. They are peaceful people. They have leaders who understand that a "balance of power" can be a preventive measure against war. Maybe another Cold War would be a good thing at this time in our history.

This I believe.

Immigrants

I wrote the following as a proposed newspaper editorial when the attitude toward immigrants darkened and Americans took to the streets in protests.

After serving three years in the service of the Austro-Hungarian Imperial Army of Franz Josef, my 20-year-old grandfather came with his new bride to America, the land of opportunity, in 1906. Margot, my well-schooled grandmother, could read the words inscribed on the Statue of Liberty before docking at Ellis Island in New York. After a 45-minute immigration process, they traveled by train to New Kensington, a mill town outside of Pittsburgh.

Both of them spoke multiple languages and fit nicely in the immigrant communities working in western Pennsylvania mills. Simon became a butcher, and the "land of opportunity" did not fail him. He soon owned his own butcher shop and prospered. His prosperity allowed him to help his siblings migrate to America and settle in nearby towns.

This family of immigrants had children who became successful based on their intelligence, strong work ethic and family values. All those immigrants contributed to their communities and the growth of their new land. Their children and grandchildren include doctors, lawyers, teachers, merchants, a justice of the peace, a judge, and many academics.

As productive and loyal Americans, they had two sons who served in the Army in WWII and sponsored new citizens escaping wartorn Eastern Europe, and two fleeing from Nazi concentration camps. They gave up a lot to share the bounty of America.

Today, my extended family of four generations keep love and respect in our hearts for our grandparents and the contributions they made to help make America great. We remember and respect the past, and will work to allow that tradition to grow for immigrants, to come and make contributions to America.

*Here I am participating in a Salem demonstration
protesting treatment of immigrants.*

be HAPPY.

seek PEACE.
give SERVICE.
be HAPPY.

WHAT *it* MEANS *to* BE HAPPY

For me, happiness is wrapped up in the people I love. Those people include family, friends from all stages of life, and of course, co-workers. This section of *Seek Peace, Give Service, Be Happy* is a celebration of the people I love – the people who helped me find peace, the people who joined me in serving humanity, and the people who just happened to walk this journey with me. It all makes me happy. The section begins with a slice of our family trip to Italy.

The Tuscan Chicken

We arrived back at the villa from La Spezia in just an hour and ten minutes. It was shortly after that that son Michael, his wife Beril, and their children, Kenan and Lucy, arrived. We were so happy to see them and to introduce them to our Tuscan retreat.

The arrival of Michael, and his Italian speaking skill, was fortuitous for another reason. When we first got back to the villa, we found a handwritten note in Italian taped to the iron entry gate. Sister-in-law-Jeanne's attempt at translation had us believing that the note was admonishing us for being loud at night.

Michael's translation relieved our fears about noise complaints and laid out a much more intriguing tale about an irritated, saddened, and sick landlord. Apparently, our landlord, Signor Aresti, had posted the notice somewhere else in the neighborhood and it was returned to our door by one of the locals. Aresti's note stated his suspicion that one of the neighbors had committed the dastardly deed of poisoning his pet chicken.

Having already been there a week, we knew this chicken. Some of us had suggested that this chicken thought it was a rooster because it tried to crow in the mornings.

Aresti's belief that a neighbor had purposely offed the chicken was a great offense to him and his family. Not only did they have *la morte de un pollo*, but Aresti was physically sick as well. Before the chicken's demise, he had eaten the last egg that it had laid. The tainted egg made Aresti ill and this magnified his anger.

As we were leaving for dinner, Aresti and Elena pulled up in their car. Michael translated as Aresti told his story and assured us that none of us were in his ring of suspicion.

Sometime that evening, Jeanne suggested that we should get Mr. Aresti another chicken. Since I had seen the young woman at the Santa Maria Visitor's Information Center answer a flurry of questions shouted at her from bewildered foreign visitors, I felt sure that her resources would yield some solid direction in my pursuit of a gift for Aresti.

Trying not to laugh aloud, I introduced my question to the most experienced of the Center's staff, beginning with a compliment. "I've observed you answering everybody's questions with great skill and authority," I said. "I have a question for you that may be unusual." She nodded. "Do you know where I can buy a chicken?" She looked at me with disbelief, then slowly dissolved into laughter. She asked for clarification.

"You want to buy some chicken to eat?"

"No, I want a live chicken. My landlord's pet chicken died, and I want to buy him a new one."

Now the others behind the counter, overhearing the bizarre question, started to laugh as well. Since my inquiry had been received in the fashion I had intended, I pumped it for all it was worth. The five young women, along with Jeanne, Sue and I, were all casting our best chicken lines.

Living up to her reputation for resourcefulness, the staffer did come up with a nearby location to buy birds. She even called to see if they also had a *gallina* (Italian for laying hen) for sale. We immediately set out for the *casa di gallina*, having promised the Center staff that we would bring the chicken back for the ladies to inspect.

We found the bird & feed store at #11 *Via Borgo Giannotti*, close to Porto Santa Maria. Caren had brought her camera to record the purchase. I had written out my request in Italian, and practiced all the way to the store. With no special note or fanfare, the clerk said "si" and went behind the store, returning with a *gallina rosso* in a cardboard box. Seven euros later, we were on our way.

First, we stopped at the Information Center to show off the hen to the ladies who had directed us to the retailer. Then, we headed home for our presentation to Aresti.

We woke him from a nap with our banging on his gate door and calling his name. Kenan, my five-year-old grandson, proudly handed the box over to the sleepy-eyed Aresti. His expression of great surprise was overtaken by tears of joy and gratitude. He gave us all big hugs and chattered on in Italian that only Michael could understand.

While having our dinner that night, under the lush grape arbor of the villa, Aresti sent his English-speaking daughter, Benedetta, down to again express his gratitude for the gift. Later in the evening, the new family addition mounted the fence between Aresti's upper-level patio and our yard. She paused only for a minute and then flew down to be with us. My interpretation was that she too wanted to thank us for uniting her with this nice family. Unafraid, she allowed me to pick her up and carry her back up to their fence. Aresti built a makeshift coop for the pet, and she remained happy.

The next day we learned that Aresti had in fact ordered a replacement chicken himself and it was delivered that day. Now, two *galline rosse* graced the villa and were headed toward the production of tasty, healthy eggs.

We saw the statue of David in Florence, the Leaning Tower at Pisa and the five picturesque villages of Cinque Terre, but the most told story of that trip was that of the Tuscan Chicken.

My Mom

I remember my mother clearly as a caring, capable, and fun woman. She was a stay-at-home mom, after being a physical education teacher after college and before marrying my dad.

In her roles as wife and mother, my mom was energetically present—every day. It was important to her that she be there when her kids came home from school. She was a good provider, warm and friendly to all our friends, a peacemaker when my older brother and I got into fights, and always eager to play with us. Even with a short career in physical education, she knew lots of games, knew how to play, threw like a boy, and shot baskets at our hoop in the driveway.

My Mom was a happy person, loving and supportive of my dad's hard work, enduring his long hours at the shop but avoiding the occasion to work there. There was a definite line of distinction in the work to be done. Dad "brought home the bacon" and she cooked it.

Speaking of cooking, honestly, she was not a highly creative cook. Meat and potatoes were our regular fare. Meat was generally "well-done."

I remember that my mom had lots of lady friends, was well-liked, did some volunteer work in the community and served on the P.T.A. at school. She was always happy and lively. She liked to sing and dance. As I got older, I understood that she liked to party - enjoyed drinking and having a wonderful time, never so much that folks would think she was tipsy, but enough to be "the life of a party."

While she had her rules, any big infractions by us kids were handed over and handled by my dad. She made sure we always did our homework. She paid attention to our report cards and any notes from teachers.

Mom was always interested and gracious about inviting our relatives to visit. Most every major holiday, we had uncles, aunts, and cousins at our house. Since dad had the butcher shop and store, we always had food. We also hosted summer reunions nearly every year, good times for all, with mom always in the center of the organization and work. Since she was the only female in her family, with five brothers, she was a special person for all our relatives' families. Many of my cousins considered her their favorite aunt.

As a young boy, a memory I have is lying on the couch with my head in her lap and her gently scratching my head. It was a good feeling and gave me a wonderful sense of security. I loved my mom and always felt her caring love for me, my brother and sister.

My Dad

I remember things about my dad that illustrate the kind of man he was. From an early age, I knew he was a hard-working person. As a retailer, his store hours were long. Six days a week from 7 A.M. to a bit after closing time, at 6 P.M. On his day off, Sundays, he did bookwork and made window signs at home.

My mother honored and respected his solid work ethic. She always praised him as a hard-working father who provided for us. I also remember little things that indicated that he was consistent. Like, on Sundays, our big meal was the midday meal, which was always meat, potatoes, and a vegetable. If that was not enough, we would fill up on bread and butter. Some Sundays, Dad would stuff us in the car and drive the back roads in Indiana County. Since our main meal was midday, the evening meal was always tea and toast. It was meager, but enjoyable, with all the things available to slather on the toast. We could choose butter and several fruit flavored jams or jellies.

After suppertime, we might make a trip to Kane's Coffee Shoppe which, for us, was an ice cream shop. Ice cream for dessert was a treat after tea and toast.

Consistently on those rides in the country, any time we passed a cemetery, he would ask, "How many dead people are in that cemetery?" When we finally stopped guessing, his answer was always, "All of them."

I also remember my dad being generous to those in need. Since he owned the meat market and small grocery store, we always had food to eat. If someone else did not have enough to eat, my dad made sure they did, and he never worried about getting paid for it. He fed the hungry, he fed the nuns at St. Bernard's convent, and he never bragged about what he'd done.

The only time I remember him complaining about customers not paying him on time was when a few who had the means to pay were slow to pay. His combined traits of generosity and fairness were evident to us.

Lucky me: Three Dads

Every Father's Day for the past sixteen years, I have shared my thanks for having had the opportunity, good fortune, and privilege to have had three great dads.

The first was my biological father, Bill Steiner. He was a wonderful dad - provider for our family, loving and good to our mother, hard-working, in service to the community where we lived, and an example to me in the many ways to grow from boyhood to adulthood. He was principled, honest, and generous. Not a highly educated person, leaving school after high school, but very smart. He was creative as a merchant and skilled as a butcher. He had followed in the footsteps of his father, who was also self-employed. I proudly say that I am a "son of a butcher." In fact, as a gift one year, I received an apron with that saying embroidered on the front.

My second dad was Joe L. Brown, father of my first wife, Cynthia, and granddad to our children Michael and Amy. Joe was a celebrity of sorts in Pittsburgh, as the General Manager of the Pittsburgh Pirates major league baseball team.

From our first meeting in 1969, Joe treated me with respect and, for the rest of his life, with a lot of love. He died at age 92, in August 2010, less than two months after he attended a reunion of the 1960 Pirates World Series Championship team. From his obituary:

> *"As the architect behind the 1960 and 1971 World Series teams, we were honored that Joe was able to return to Pittsburgh in June to help us celebrate the 50th anniversary. The ovation he received prior to the game was a special moment for Joe and his family.*

Brown, the son of famed comedian Joe E. Brown, succeeded Branch Rickey as the Pirates' General Manager following a last-place season in 1955. He stayed on the job through 1976, a span in which the Pirates won the 1960 and 1971 World Series and five National League East titles."

Joe treated me like a son. He was generous, fun-loving, self-assured as a public figure, and intimate as a private, family person. He was devoted to his children, Cynthia, and Don (Ty) and fond and proud of his only grandchildren, Michael, and Amy. The true love he continued to show and express following my divorce from Cynthia was a gift beyond measure. He also was generous with his affection for the woman I married next, Caren Ann.

Not all people have the good fortune of having one great dad, I have had the unbelievable good fortune to now have a third - Wilton Jackson. Wilton, father of Caren Ann and seven other children, was different in some ways from my first two dads, but certainly important to me, as a man to be respected and loved.

Wilton, devoted to his wife Margery for 76 years, was a successful businessperson and a generous community leader. His childhood was not without sadness or sorrow, including the abandonment of his family by his father. The adversity was perhaps a motivating factor, as Wilton succeeded in every job with grit, guile, grace, hard work, and good humor.

Wilton was a guiding star for his family and community, first in Nyssa, in the wild, northeast corner of Oregon, and for his final two decades, across the state in Mary's Woods' retirement village, located in suburban Lake Oswego. During those last 20 years, Wilton was a treasure for me. I learned some new things from him and was also reminded of lessons learned from my other two dads.

Wilton charmed me with his character, decency, good humor, and devotion to family. His love and devotion to Margery was a story for the ages. After his 100th birthday and Margery's failing health, he continued to calm her by singing You are My Sunshine.

Margery died on February 13th, 2021, on the eve of Valentine's Day, knowing she was floating up to heaven. With his earthly care-giving job completed, Wilton followed her to their eternal resting place three days later.

Lessons learned from my three "dads," leave me truly blessed.

My Steiner Grandparents

My father, Bill, standing at the back, on the right. His other siblings, from left to right in the front: Arnold, Emory and Alice.

The interesting things that I know and remember about my grandparents were mostly learned as a middle-aged adult. There were many memories from my childhood days, but the good and juicy things came when I was old enough to better understand and appreciate the stories.

I'll start on the Steiner side of the family. Simon Steiner came to the United States in 1906, after serving his obligatory military commitment in the army of Austro-Hungarian Emperor Franz Josef. Simon had a sweetheart, Margot Brauer, who waited patiently for him to matriculate out of the service and head for the promised land, America. Both Simon and Margot (later referred to as Margaret) were Jewish. She and her family were much more devout in their faith than Simon was.

I know little of Grandma Steiner's (Margot Brauer) family and whether she had more than a younger sibling, Ben. But Simon had four or five brothers and two sisters. He was the oldest, with our Uncle Julius next. There was an Uncle Louis, who left his wife, Uncle Arpod, who stole money from his employer's bank and spent some time in prison, and my favorite, the youngest brother, Uncle Emil.

My knowledge of the sister siblings was limited to seeing some old photographs of the group of them after they all came to America. Grandpa was a butcher by trade when he came to the U.S. I do not know if his father was a butcher, if he learned as an apprentice of another, or if he learned the trade in the service. So, my father could also claim to be the son of a butcher.

It is reported in family records and immigration documents that Simon came to this country through Ellis Island in New York. I don't know why they continued to New Kensington, Pennsylvania, but they settled in the shadow of the huge Pittsburgh Plate Glass (PPG) factory. He had his own butcher shop at an early age and thrived. Much of his early success was due to his ability to speak so many different languages. When they left Europe, that part of the continent was at odds with each other, with borders changing to a point that they, at any given time, were not sure if they were Hungarian, Austrian, German, Polish, Czech or Russian. The Steiners seemed to want to stick to the story that they were Hungarian. Anyway, with all the moving, changing borders, different governments, and his attending different schools, Simon learned to speak, read, and write in most of those languages.

At the PPG factory, the laborers came from all those countries, as did their wives, mothers, and children. All of them were customers at Steiner's Butcher Shop. Customers then had more trust in people who could speak to them in their native tongues. Not only did my grandfather meet his customers in his store, he regularly went out to find new and additional customers in small coal mining towns outside of New Kensington and Pittsburgh. All the area factories needed coal to fuel the huge belching furnaces that burned day and night.

In a horse-drawn wagon, his un-cut chunks of meat covered by a tarp, and a bugle on the bench seat beside him, he went from town to nearby town to sell his locally grown beef, pork, and chickens. To announce his presence in the town square or near the coal company paymaster's booth, a few blasts on the bugle heralded that he and his meat were there and open for business.

From several pictures that I have seen, my grandfather was a very handsome man. With his white shirt, necktie, and trimmed mustache, he cut a handsome figure. Not that there were chances to be unfaithful to Margaret, but he always took opportunities to flirt with the ladies. While their men were digging coal below ground, the ladies frolicked with the butcher with the bugle.

In a short number of years, Steiner's market became successful and my grandfather, generally full of himself and his success, was not hesitant to boast. He used his success to afford a large degree of largess, and he helped his younger siblings come to the "promised land" of America.

With pockets full of money and the bursting pride of business success, Simon boarded a steamship headed back to the "old country" sometime in the middle of July, 1914. His plan was to visit Margot's family and brag about how high they lived in America, then encourage the rest of the family to quickly follow them to the banks of the Allegheny River. He told them about the reasonable wages earned by laborers, how those wages were sufficient to support growing families, and how many of them were his customers at Steiner's Market.

Unbeknownst to him while on the ship, the Austro-Hungarian Emperor, Franz Josef, was assassinated, which sparked the start of World War I between the middle European countries and Germany. Simon knew nothing of this news when he arrived at the Brauer home. In a panic, his mother-in-law, our great grandmother, pushed their son Ben into Simon's arms, pleading with him "you must go back and take Ben with you." At that moment, the boasting butcher became a hurried hero.

Grandpa Steiner, in spite of a business career of boom or bust, was always a jovial man with countless friends.

What I remember about my grandmother is all wonderful. Smart, classy, gracious, generous and a world-class cook. Her meals were legendary - outshined only by the generous way that she was willing to share the wealth of her kitchen. Classic Hungarian cooking, crowned by her baking. Christmas cookies, despite the fact the Steiners did not celebrate Christmas, were shared with all.

In the final years of his life, Grandpa Steiner became a peddler out of the trunk of his car. Somewhere in Pittsburgh he purchased shirts, socks, and underwear. Without a storefront, he again used his jovial personality, his language skills, and friendships to make a little money and be financially independent. His sales routes were familiar, the same coal mining towns that he visited years ago when his cart followed a horse.

On occasions, when his town-to-town itinerary got close to my hometown of Indiana, he would stop to visit. Sometimes Grandma was with him, and always something came out of the car's trunk and into my bedroom.

I learned Grandpa Steiner had a big personality and was somewhat full of himself. He also had the wonderful good fortune of having a family surrounding him.

At one point, his butcher shop was doing very well in New Kensington, near Pittsburgh. Despite the success, he was always dreaming and scheming of ways to do better. Unlike the European style of shopping daily, he was amazed at the larger format retailers like Murphy's Five and Ten Cent stores. There was a large Murphy's store in downtown Pittsburgh.

Murphy's had a large selection of merchandise, located on Fifth Avenue downtown, right on the streetcar line that went east to the Hill District and then to Oakland and Wilkinsburg. That first neighborhood, the Hill District, was populated primarily with Italian families, the first arrivals in the land of plenty.

Murphy's Five and Ten Cent store was forerunner of the Walmart stores of today. Grandpa's concept was to put a butcher shop right on the main floor of Murphy's store. Folks living downtown could shop, jump on the streetcar, and take their evening meal home with them.

Grandpa went to McKeesport, the headquarters of Murphy's. The brass liked his idea, leased a space to him near the main entrance, set up the butcher shop in a sea of hard goods, and it was an immediate success.

Very soon afterward, Grandpa Simon moved the family to a more fashionable section of Pittsburgh, East Liberty, bought a big fancy car, and strutted around with great pride.

Soon after this great triumph, he was driving his big fancy car when he caused an accident that killed the daughter of a prominent Pittsburgh industrialist. Lawsuits followed and grandpa lost his new fortune.

Another story floats through the family, about his creative nature and his alleged inventions. The most prominent one had him inventing brake lights for automobiles. His plowing into the rear of the industrialist's car probably inspired this. Unfortunately, the design engineers at Ford Motor Company in Detroit had already developed brake lights for automobiles before grandpa got his into production and on the market.

Disappointed but never defeated, grandpa had great spirit, humor, and self-assurance.

My Patrizio Grandparents

I remember my grandmother, Anna Patrizio, vividly. She was sweet and beloved by all her grandchildren. As a youngster, I remember her as a frequent visitor to our house in Pennsylvania. After each visit, we could always count on a dollar being deposited under the pillows of each of our beds.

She lived alone in a big house, with terrazzo floors, on 8th Street in Oakmont, about an hour west of us. Although the house was large, attractive, and comfortable, it was always dimly lit and cold. As a child, I did not know why she was unhappy, but the terrazzo floors probably reminded her of our grandfather, Giovanni Patrizio, who left her for another woman. Grandma Patrizio lived until she was 93. My last memories of her were those last couple of years when I was going to law school at night, and I would visit her as often as I could.

Giovanni was a successful construction contractor dealing in terrazzo and marble. I have only one memory of seeing him in person. Once, I must have been five or six years old, my mother had taken us to Pittsburgh to shop. Giovanni's combination office-garage-shop was on 5th Avenue, near downtown, in what became the Hill District. Way back then, it was close to where most of the Italian immigrants lived. Gradually, the Italians moved east to East Liberty and eventually Penn Hills.

Giovanni had helped bring the workers from the Freuli area of Italy to work for him. When skilled worker earned enough money, they brought their families over and settled near the shop.

I remember on one occasion, visiting him in the shop and him giving me me a box of Toronni candy. That candy became an annual Christmas gift, which was a reminder that we did have a grandfather,

My grandfather (back row, fourth from left) with his employees, three of them his brothers. Also in the back row (third from left) is Primo Carnera, heavyweight champion of the world for a year (1933 – 34), who was from the same small town in Italy where the Patrizio family once lived.

not loved and known, but he and the candy continued until I was about fourteen, when he died. I never understood why a grandfather would leave his wife, six children and twelve lovable grandchildren.

Eulogy for Brother Bill

What words does one choose to share about Bill? As I prepared for this task, words like family, hard work, love, fun, and son of a butcher came to mind.

I asked family members what words most resonated for them. The lexicon then expanded as they offered words like safe, devoted, touchstone, integrity, committed and caring.

To borrow a phrase from Willa Cather, in her book *Death Comes for The Archbishop*, Bill did not die of cancer. He died of living. Living a good life.

Living a full life.

*Living a life full of love in the arms of his high
school sweetheart.*

*Living a life surrounded by his children and wonderfully
talented grandchildren.*

*Living a life of hard work that earned him the respect
of construction people all over the country, and local
renters in their modest apartments and duplexes.*

Using some of those words that resonated, let me start with family. Bill and Jean created a wonderfully unique and loving family. The examples that our parents and Jean's parents set were sterling foundations.

Speaking of unique families reminds me of the time a few years back when Caren and I went to Mass at the Newman Center on the campus of the University of New Mexico. It happened to be the Feast of the Holy Family, and Father George was the celebrant. Father George was well into his 80's and was a very energetic, and at times, irreverent Dominican. Anyway, his sermon was about the fact that Catholics were called to be tolerant of all sorts of families. Single parents, mixed marriages, and mixed race families were all to be accepted as equals. He went on to say that this Feast of the Holy Family is a time to focus on this message: "Look at the Holy Family," Father George said, "the father is an old man, his wife is a teen virgin, and the kid thinks he is God."

Let me take you back for a moment to our growing up in the small town of Indiana, Pennsylvania. The Secosky family and the Steiner family lived fairly close, and the kids were in school together. The Secoskys had one son and four daughters who were all bright, good looking, and popular.

The town and the school were small enough that most people knew each other and sometimes knew each other's business. The high school math teacher, Laura Church, played the role of cupid to encourage Jean (Secosky) to give some consideration to going out with Bill, my brother. Miss Church had observed him in her class, gazing into space, daydreaming about the beautiful, lively cheerleader and classroom star. Jean agreed, and that was the start of a love affair, and a wonderful marriage that lasted more than five decades.

One of my early memories of their courtship was seeing them riding in dad's 1954 orange Ford Skyliner. Cars had bench seats then. On a date, most girls sat so close to the boy driving that she was almost in his lap. But Jean, being ultra-cool, sat next to the door. As the younger, 13-year-old brother, I thought she was the best.

That high school romance, and their 56-year marriage, led to a wonderful family, all growing in their love and devotion to each other.

Having all four of their children and their grandchildren living so close has been a blessing for Bill and Jean, and a blessing for their offspring. The children and grandchildren continued to receive the benefits of parental love, guidance, learning, wisdom, good home cooking, and the moral and spiritual guidance that comes from a loving couple.

Brother Joe's word was "safe." Joe shared with me the story about when his son Max died. Bill was out of town on a business trip. Cutting it short, he came home to comfort and support Joe, who was enduring his darkest hour. Joe told me that when he saw his dad walk into the room, he immediately felt safe. Feeling safe is a learned emotion. Only those of us lucky enough to have had good, supportive, nurturing parents or caregivers can enjoy the benefit of that limbic feeling of safety.

Christina's word was "devoted." Devoted is what Bill and Jean have been. Devoted to their children and grandchildren through thick and thin. Using "thick and thin" is a safe way to illustrate devotion, and an effective way to avoid going into a lot of detail about occasions and experiences that are now distant memories, sometimes better forgotten. Christina continues the trait of devotion to her two girls, Payton and Canon, and her husband Robert.

Robert's word was "committed." Robert and his two children have been a wonderful addition to the family in the past year. Bill's commitment extended to all the children's spouses and their families. Robert's word, committed, was also evident throughout his life. When he says he will do something, join a team or a group or do someone a favor, his commitment is as good as gold.

Payton selected "caring" as a word to characterize and honor her grandfather. He expressed his caring in all the ways that a good granddad does: attending performances, sporting events, asking about school grades and friendships. Bill did care and showed it to all his family members and friends.

It took Canon two words to best describe her grandfather: "amazing, incredible." We should all be so lucky to receive these kinds of reviews. Playing this word game is also a good reminder that, if we think these things about a loved one, why wait until their funeral to say them aloud?

Sister Sue, who Bill referred to as his baby sister, offered the word "touchstone." A touchstone is a black stone used to test the purity of gold and silver. It provides a test of genuineness. Bill was certainly genuine. One always knew where he was on any subject. Nothing fake about him. A solid moral compass always guided his positions.

Bill stayed out of controversy, but a little-known story shows how, without knowing it, he was a great peacemaker. When our parents married, there was a great tumult because the son of a Jewish family was marrying an Italian Catholic girl. Our Jewish grandparents were livid. They were livid until Bill, their first grandchild, was born. He brought peace to the family. To their credit, Grandma and Grandpa Steiner treated our mother with total love and respect for the rest of their lives.

Bill's anointment as the peacemaker did not last. When I came along, Bill had to share the attention of adoring parents, grandparents, aunts, and uncles. He was not at all pleased. There is one old family photo that shows three-year-old Billy Ray with infant Ronny. He has me in a headlock while gritting his teeth.

To distinguish little Bill from our dad, also named Bill, the family used his middle name, and he was called Billy Ray. As he grew older, he did not like that very much. Our cousin Dolly told me she was one of the few people he allowed to call him Billy Ray. Then Jean and Bill did the same thing to son number one, and now the very grown-up Bill Steiner (the third) does not like the name any more than his dad did.

Back to the mention of a good moral compass, the word that young Bill offered up is "integrity." This is a word that Bill lived his life by, and it is certainly one that he and Jean passed on to their children. Integrity is sometimes quantified as the worth that we place on ourselves. We become the measure of truth. We become our own measures of honesty. We become the definition of loyalty. If we were to cheat on a business contract or steal something, the amount of that gain is what we see as our self-worth. The ability to hold and keep confidence is a measure of integrity. Bill lived his life with a moral compass, made with integrity.

Melissa's word for her dad was "warrior." He demonstrated those traits often, never more bravely than in his last months. He fought with great dignity, as a brave warrior would.

Rob's word was "patriarch." Bill was respected, proud, and robust in support of his offspring.

Mitch chose "supportive" as his word. We saw that play out recently as Mitch earned the opportunity to gain an appointment to the Air Force Academy. Bill was supportive of Mitch's efforts and proud of his achievements.

Luke saw his grandfather as "enterprising." Bill certainly was that. All his working life, he figured out how to take the next step, take the next risk, develop the next great idea and he succeeded as his own man every time. That enterprising attitude required great energy, smart moves, and a lot of demanding work.

Work does come to mind. Bill's business, installing arena dividers, produces structures that are, as Cousin Amy referred to them, monuments to his work. Some of those monuments are right here in Indianapolis, at Lucas Oil Stadium, the home of the Colts. Some of the other dividers are found in the FedEx Arena in Memphis, the Moda Center in Portland, Veterans Memorial Coliseum in Nashville, the Barclay Center in Brooklyn, and arenas on the campuses of Penn State, and the Universities of Michigan and Oregon.

When Bill was 65, I asked him if he was considering retiring or quitting work. His reply was typical Bill: "No, I don't ever want to quit." He made that a reality, continuing to work as much as his energy allowed during the months of his cancer treatment. It was within a week of his death that he finally gave it up, writing a letter to his associates in New York telling them he could not go on.

Bill was known by all, even well into his 70's, as a hard worker. It was commonplace to find him climbing a ladder in the rigging near the roof of one of his arena jobs or crawling under a sink at one of his rentals, fixing a leaky pipe. We believe he got that trait from our father. Bill and I did not learn how to fish, hunt or camp as kids. But we did learn how to work.

I like to learn and use unfamiliar words. One that I learned just this week is "aphorism." An aphorism is a short, pointed statement expressing a wise observation. An apt aphorism we might use to wind up this eulogy is "We knew him." Bill was blessed in his life with love and family, respect and recognition for who he was and what he stood for. We knew him and we know how to remember him. In honor of his life, let us remember to tell those we love that we love them. Let us tell those we respect that we respect them. Let us tell those who make us feel safe that we appreciate them.

Bill, may you rest in peace and in our lasting sweet memories of you.

Uncle Arnold's Eulogy

Arnold did not die because of heart failure. He died because he lived.

He lived nearly a century, longer than anyone I ever knew. He died about eight months short of his goal to reach 100. "Short of his goal" was by no means the measure of his life. Because he DID live. He lived a big life. Not always sunshine and lollipops, but you would never know he had days of sadness and fear.

Arnold lived a special life he created with his intellect, his charm, his grace, his sense of humor, his integrity, and his arms stretched out to make others feel good.

Arnold lived a life that knew love. He had the love and admiration of two wonderful women, Lillian, and Rayetta. He had the love of a son and daughter, Richard gone much too young, and Becky who was with him through his dying moments.

Arnold lived a life full of spirit and enthusiasm, whether it be a game of bridge, Scrabble, travel, telling a joke, meeting an old friend, enjoying a visit from one of the scores of people he trained in his work, or from his former boss, or from an Army buddy, or from a niece or nephew, or from the people to whom he and Rayetta taught English as a second language. They became family too. Arnold unfailingly shared his charm, humor, and good grace.

Part of that good grace was his natural sense of inquiry. Conversations with Arnold were never just about him. He was always interested to hear about others. He asked questions with real meaning, and he desired to actually hear the answers. Delighted by the accomplishments of others, he made people feel that they were heard.

It was Will Rogers who said he never met a man he didn't like, but it was Arnold who lived that life, being someone who liked everyone and was therefore liked by everyone.

Recently, when we visited Arnold on his 99th birthday, we were introduced to one of his newest friends, someone from his new residence. The new friend pointed to Arnold with great gusto and said, "This guy is a real sweetheart." And Arnold was that, a sweetheart for friends of many decades as well as for his newest acquaintances.

We will miss Arnold and we have sweet memories of this sweetheart of a man. To fulfill the dreams of youth is the best that can happen to a man. Arnold lived that sort of life and he also set a standard for all of us to try to emulate.

On that 99th birthday visit, I witnessed Arnold sipping a glass of vodka and orange juice. I told him, "I'm happy to see you are still enjoying your drink." He replied, "I drink to make me happy, not you." But just the way he said it did make me happy. I'll always hold that memory, because Arnold was a man who lived his life to the fullest and made others happy to know and love him.

Old Friends, Good Friends, Good People

The Celebration of Life Model

I recently participated in a book discussion group on *The Inner Work of Age: Shifting from Role to Soul*. It features lessons in aging. It occurred to me that there is another meaning for a celebration of life event. When one of the discussion group members spoke about her mother during her final months on earth, she said her mother was angry and unpleasant to most. I had been at her mother's celebration of life event and I never heard anything like that. Nothing but sweet memories!

It dawned on me that so many people say nice things about friends after they're gone rather than face-to-face while they are still here. Therefore, I developed an idea to push myself to tell all the people I care for what they mean to me.

While they are still with us.

I am not doing this to solicit positive comments about me from these friends. The absolute opposite is true because it will give me the opportunity to tell them how I feel about them while I am still able to do so. I'll be giving, not receiving, the positive comments.

As I get closer to my own demise, it becomes important that I do this in the right order.

For me, this is a better way to celebrate life.

The first step will be to comb through all my lists: telephone numbers, mailing addresses, birthdays – anything I have that includes those friends I care about. Then, I will begin a regular process of reaching out to them. I am not thinking everything I will say is going to be sweet sloppy bouquets. It is more likely going to be remembering fun experiences we had together.

My Sister Sue

I understand that I was not the best older brother for Sue, since it took a long time for her to trust me or to play with me. We both grew up on Locust Street, in Indiana, PA. We had lots of friends in the neighborhood and played, and played, and played. There are two occasions that she remembered, at age 81, when we gathered to reminisce.

The first story she remembered - and I unfortunately remembered as well - was a trick called "Does a match burn twice?" I was the culprit; she was the victim.

I said, "Does a match burn twice?" Then I lit a match, blew it out, then placed it on her tummy. She certainly witnessed a match burning twice, went crying to our mother, who made sure I did not pull that joke again... anywhere. Remembering the story still chills my bones.

The second story (photo) is another case of my unkindness to Sue: suffice it to say I was the robber who kidnapped a young victim. I am relieved that she has no memory of this.

I guess I was following the example of our older brother Bill, three years my senior, who beat the crap out of me until I was 19 years old. Our parents didn't like it, but they didn't do a thing about it, like sending him to reform school.

Me and my prisoner, sister Sue.

Based on our 2023 conversation, Sue allowed that she started to like me when I was in ninth grade, playing football. It brought us closer that during one of our freshman games, I got "kicked where it counts" and had to go to bed for five days. Sue reminded me that, "Mother would have both of our lunches ready when I got home from school. I would carry them upstairs and we would have lunch together." I was too incapacitated to tease her; it was a good time for us to be nice to each other and move forward into a better relationship.

After that rocky start, we came to love each other very much and have stayed in touch, behaving favorably with each other and one another's families. When we all lived in Pittsburgh, everyone had lots of fun with our children all together. Sue and her husband, Tom, had Krista, Jacqueline, and Stefan, - about the same ages as our two, Michael and Amy. Then there was a gap of about eight years, until Kaaren came along. Our combined families were famously known as the Steinpacks, a combination of our surnames.

The kids had so much fun performing plays, skits, and comedy routines. All of them had great senses of humor. Amy developed her improv in college and Kaaren developed her own creativity as a nightclub singer, artist, and hairstylist as she entered adulthood.

Sue has seven grandchildren, all of them girls.

We do not talk much about Tom, since she and Tom divorced years ago. Tom was a very talented architect. He passed away and Sue moved to Pleasant Ridge, a Detroit suburb. She's acquired an assortment of nicknames: "G-ma", "swim-team super-fan" and "neighborhood gardener".

When I was in 11th grade, at Indiana Junior High School, and Sue was a 9th grader, we went to dances at the school gym and teen center, doing the jitterbug as much as we could. It was great fun; she was a great dancer, and I was learning as I went along. Most of the girls liked her, as well as the boys. She was growing out of the phase of girls being jealous of one another, into a mature, well-mannered young lady. She got all As, participated in clubs and activities and became a cheerleader for the varsity teams when she was in 10th grade. I do not remember this, but she might have qualified as an "accomplished" high school student.

She started her college years at Mercyhurst College and found it too small, without any sophistication, and having too much bad weather. The school was in Erie, Pennsylvania, the town known as the "mistake on the lake." At the end of her first year, she transferred to Carnegie Mellon University in Pittsburgh, choosing the bigger city, more excitement, and a curriculum that included fashion and merchandising.

After her divorce, Sue took a job with a lot of responsibility as an office manager for the Combustion Engineers Institute. She was dealing with very few office mates and a very large group of college professors, engineers, and scientists. She did such a fabulous job, in the office and with the membership of the Institute. As she built her reputation, the membership also grew.

Part of her responsibility was to plan, administer, and host the Institute's national and international annual conferences. This included lots of international travel that allowed her to connect with spouses of members, friends and other world-wide travelers, and people that were used to visiting sophisticated locations.

During the years Sue was married, she did not receive the benefit of support and endorsement from her husband as a capable professional. But later on, the members of the Institute valued her ability and accomplishments. In fact, one of her Ivy League professor/colleagues finally helped her to see that she was accomplished and worthy of great things. For example, for many years, Sue was the executive director of the Point Park Pittsburgh Art Show, one of the leading public events of the eastern United States. As a community leader and the Institute's point person, she gained recognition and respect as a volunteer and a world-wide professional.

It took a while for Sue to like me and now I think she loves me, as I love her. My little sister is as accomplished as anyone among us.

Bunny & Merritt

I remember it very well. August 1966. You returned to work after your wedding celebration, and I showed up for my first day of work at the station. This year (2020) it will be 54 years that we have been friends - highly valued friends.

Steeler football games. Drinks at the Encore in Shadyside. Many parties with bunches of crazy people and more than one New Year's Eve featuring a new calendar with hilarious pictures.

We worked together at WIIC-TV and, after 13 years, I left the station for a difficult experience in Toledo. Sometime later, you (Merritt) started to climb the corporate ladder, so you were moving up and making a name for yourself.

While there in Pittsburgh, we partied a lot and enjoyed our Friday lunches at Tambellini's on 4th Street, followed by Silver Bullets at the Press Club. It must have been a very easy business, because we were silly when we returned to the office. Bunny, you must have driven that orange Nash home on many of those Friday nights.

Years later, you visited us in Albuquerque for the International Balloon Festival and art shopping on Canyon Road in Santa Fe.

Sometime later, Caren Ann and I visited you in Asheville where we took the comedic bus tour, had a great meal in your beautiful apartment full of wonderful art, and enjoyed the drumming from Parkside below. "Enjoyed" may not have been Bunny's word for it.

I feel so blessed to have such wonderful friends as you two. I love you both for the years of friendship, Bunny's outstanding penmanship, and Merritt's business updates. You are outstanding friends that I am very proud to have in my life. All class and A1!

As an aside, I appreciate that you have been able to keep friendships going with both of my wives. That made things so much easier for me. Best wishes for the rest of your lives.

Peace,

Ron

Jack Delaney

The one remaining childhood and high school friend that I know about, and have kept in touch with, is Jack Delaney. Jack was a year behind me in high school. His older brother, Danny, was in my class. Dan left eighth grade after our mid-school years at St. Bernard's School and went to the seminary, wanting to be a priest. That lasted less than two years and he joined us during our IJHS 10th grade year.

There were four Delaney boys: Danny, Jack, Jimmy, and Tom. A younger sister came last and, sadly, soon after her birth, their mother died. The infant girl was taken to DuBois, PA, to be raised by an aunt and uncle.

Jack, his brothers and I were friends as young kids, playing games in each other's yards in summer, and in basements in cold and snowy winters.

We became close when both of us were young, married, and living in Pittsburgh. I was working at WIIC-TV, the NBC affiliate there. Jack had gone to college some, spent a tour in the Navy, and returned to western PA. He was married to Susan, a graduate from Indiana University of Pennsylvania.

An interesting and strange name, but the town was Indiana, the state was Pennsylvania, and Jack and I were both "townies," guys who lived in town and chased after girls from the local university.

The two things that brought us together in those days in Pittsburgh were mutual friends, Don and Roseann Fusina, and Highland Country Club where we played golf together.

Jack had a great personality and was smart, in a lot of ways. He started selling cars for Beriel Chevrolet, in the North Hills of Pittsburgh. He evidently was an outstanding seller of cars and a builder of relationships with all the right people. As I remember the story, Mr. Beriel helped Jack finance and buy the old and tired Chevy dealership on Water Street, in Indiana.

Jack and Susan had three wonderful kids, Jack Jr., Tom, and Beth. Jack grew the dealership, which became plural when Honda was added. Later, there were additional auto brands. Then Jack Jr. and Tommy joined the business. Susan was always a partner, bookkeeper, outstanding mother, and community leader. Daughter Beth is now a lawyer and mother, living back in Indiana and doing the legal work for the dealerships.

Today, Delaney Auto Group has dealerships in Indiana, Greensburgh (PA), Pittsburgh and recently added new dealerships in State College, PA.

Jack has changed in many ways since high school - in wealth, the number of golf clubs he belongs to, in wonderful grandchildren that he and Susan proudly enjoy, and in the high stature he enjoys in the towns where he does business.

Despite all this, Jack is the same person that I have known all my life. More gray hair, but no less fun. More business connections, but still holding dear with his many high school friends who have stayed and prospered back in Indiana, PA. Thoughtful and warm, and though we see each other seldom, Jack remembers to catch up with a long holiday phone call. He is a true friend.

Lost Too Soon

Over the course of my life, I've been blessed with very nice friends. Some of them were friends for many, many years. Unfortunately, some died before their time. I miss them still. Losing my grandparents, who were quite elderly at the time of their passing, was one thing, but those that left too soon was entirely another.

Eddie Konrad

The first friend that I lost was Eddie Konrad. We met in the seventh grade on a basketball court at St. Mary's Parish, in Arnold, PA.

The basketball game, and the meeting, was set up by Father Francis Lesniac, who was transferred to Indiana's St. Bernard's Parish. He was to serve as the assistant to the stern and conservative pastor, Fr. James Brady.

Father Francis was a link to sports, as well as a link to my Catholic upbringing. He loved to play sports and be around parish kids who wanted to play. Coaching or just playing, Father Francis was in his joy. Soon after his arrival in Indiana, he arranged a basketball game between the two churches' seventh grade teams.

Following the first game at St. Mary's, we went to Eddie's house for some refreshments, and met Eddie's parents, and sister Rosemary. They were a lovely, warm, and welcoming family who treated us very well.

On the return engagement of the two teams, which was held in Indiana, the St. Mary's squad and coaches were all invited to our house where my mother put together a spread for the visiting team and our team. The same thing happened the next season. Eddie and I hit it off well, and the friendships were encouraged by both families and Fr. Francis.

The following summer, we invited Eddie to come to our house for a week's vacation and then, later in the summer, I did the same, visiting his home and family.

The friendship between Eddie and me grew over the next high school years. When I decided to go to Allegheny College in Meadville, Eddie decided to go to Cannon College, in nearby Erie. We kept in touch with a few phone calls and letters - occasionally visiting each other's campus. I remember on one occasion, he came down with a carload of girls from Mercyhurst College for one of my football games.

Soon after college, Eddie met a girl. They fell in love, married quickly and had two children. He was soon beset with a strange and uncommon malady - something that affected his neck, head, and brain. I was concerned for him but not schooled enough to imagine his malady was life-threatening.

When Eddie first visited the hospital, he had a stint put in his neck which allowed the fluids to flow more swiftly between his body and brain. Unfortunately, that malady caused his decline. Before long, with a young wife and two small children, Eddie tragically died.

I tried the best I could, trying to keep in touch with his widow, but she eventually moved on with her life and I haven't heard anything about her since.

When I now think about Eddie, and my letting a friendship that we had in our teenage and college years languish, I carry some shame for my inability to stay in touch with his family. My naïve and undeveloped self failed them and me. I lost a good friend and have only this story to share.

Frank Maldonado

I met Frank Maldonado at the Allegheny College preseason football camp in 1957. Small-town freshman Ron meets big-city upperclassman. I knew only one family of color among the 10,000 residents of Indiana, PA. That was my dad's friend Sherman Scofield, owner of the local garbage company. So, here I was in college, meeting a very cool-looking guy from New York City, who happened to be the very first Puerto Rican I ever met.

The first exercise of the first day of Allegheny football pre-season workouts was to run a full mile around the track. Bobby Adams, another freshman, and I were the only ones to finish the mile without stopping, gasping for breath, and walking the last number of yards to the finish line.

The upperclassmen were all smiling and seemed satisfied to fail Coach Moore's "first request". Frank, who was standing near me said, "Hey kid, don't worry. That was the coach's little joke on all the freshmen. No one was expected to run the full mile without stopping. Nice going."

That was the first of countless acts of kindness, friendship, and brotherhood that Frank shared with me for the next two years of college, and for many years that followed.

Another of the first favors that Frank extended was introducing me to one of his fraternity brothers, Bill Henry, from nearby Brookville, about 40 miles from my hometown. Bill was on the school golf team. He was a good all-around athlete, and he had a car on campus.

99

In the second semester of my freshman year, Frank and Bill started to share with me the process of "fraternity rush." Most of the members of the football team belonged to the Phi Gam house and some assumed I would join their house. The Phi Gam members I got to know didn't fit as well as my two new friends at the Phi Kappa Psi house.

During the spring term, Frank was on the varsity baseball team and Bill on the golf team. We still had time to get together and work out at the gym, which was across the side street from the Phi Psi house. We would also meet up at the nearby Student Union, where Bill taught me to play bridge and Frank introduced me to some of the co-eds in his class. This was a very nice favor, one of many.

During that spring semester, I turned 19 and thought it was time to learn how to drink beer. Bill would drive Frank and me down to Catalano's Bar, south of downtown Meadville, for a few beers.

Spring semester was also official Rush Weeks. I attended a few parties at both the Phi Gam and Phi Psi houses. Between those parties and Catalano's, I learned that the more moderate beer beer-drinking style of Frank and his brothers was more my style. So, I pledged Phi Psi and Frank signed on as my "big brother."

Another early introduction was to Stu Sherman, one year ahead of my class, hailing from New York City, and someone who I admired immediately as a good Phi Psi.

Nearly 20 years after graduation, Stu and I hooked up again when I moved to Albuquerque. Along with his wife Rosalie, they became great friends and introduced our family to the city and many among their long list of friends.

Moving into the Phi Psi house my sophomore year allowed me to hang out with Frank, Bill, and the other brothers. We would go to the third floor to listen to Frank Sinatra records, learn more about fraternity living, and enjoy some great bonding.

My very first trip to Broadway was thanks to Frank, when he introduced the two small town boys to New York cheesecake, Hell's Kitchen, an outside view of Yankee Stadium and Madison Square Garden, subways, and his wonderful mother, who raised him and his sister as a single mother working in a garment factory.

As a youngster, Frank spent much of his time at the local Boys & Girls Club. He learned a lot there, and contributed much to ball teams and the club's neighborhood newspaper. He was an eighth grader when an uptown lawyer read one of Frank's newspaper articles, sought him out, and became a mentor, supporting Frank's decision to go to Allegheny. This was a magnificent gesture that was repaid many times over, in Frank's many generosities to all sorts of people throughout his lifetime.

After my "big brother" graduated in 1959, we were able to stay in touch. I bounced around from job to job after my graduation. I quit my third job in three years to go to night law school, at Duquesne University. Once again, Frank came to my aid by giving me a place to live above his beer distributor business. I had a job at a gas station he owned, loading and unloading beer trucks during the day and on weekends. I got to know one of the most colorful *Damon Runyan*-type characters in all of Pittsburgh, his partner in business, Joe Litman.

Joe knew, and sold beer to, many of the most famous and infamous bars and restaurants in the city, while Frank did the inside work of running a successful beer distributorship.

Years later, Frank and I kept in touch, including six or seven trips to the annual Toronto Film Festival. Frank and his wife, Angela, Bill and Malinda Henry, Ray Becki and Caren Ann and I would devour three or four movies, along with a wonderful ethnic meal at one of Toronto's long list of great restaurants. We did this for five or six straight days.

Frank Maldonado was a cherished friend, passing away too soon. He certainly made my college years better, and continued to share his gifts and favors throughout his life. I will always remember him as one of my best friends.

Andy Kuzneski

I was keeping up with one of my very best friends, Andy Kuzneski, who unexpectedly, and sadly, passed away several years ago at age 53. Andy was a strapping farm boy with three brothers. He was the son of a second-generation Polish potato farmer, who also died at an early age of a faulty heart.

Andy was big in stature. A big personality. A smile as broad as Philadelphia Street, the main drag in Indiana, PA. Andy had a big circle of friends, and a big reputation. He was tall, but I don't think I ever had a friend who was larger in life than Andy Kuzneski.

We met on the football field. He was a freshman, and I was a sophomore at Indiana Joint High School. Andy was the center, and my position was quarterback.

Andy moved up to varsity football when I was a junior. That was the year Indiana won the Western Pennsylvania High School Football Championship trophy.

I went to a small college (Allegheny), while Andy went to a big-time football college, the University of Pittsburgh. In those years, Pitt, Penn State, and Syracuse were the three best college football programs in the east. Andy made first-string when he was a junior at Pitt, which earned him a big-time reputation in small-town Indiana and Indiana County.

The story of Andy's recruitment by Pitt was somewhat legendary.

For his first recruiting interview with the Pitt coaches, Andy wore two sweatshirts underneath his dad's sport coat. No one can be sure if it was the extra heft of the sweatshirts or Andy's enthusiastic demeanor that convinced those coaches to recruit him.

After college, Andy's teammates, Mike Ditka and Ralph Conrad, went on to the pros and Andy went back to Indiana, PA to sell insurance with Penn Mutual Life Insurance Company. He was a natural salesperson, and a good friend.

Andy and I spent a lot of time together in those early years, hanging around Pittsburgh.

His mom was a second-generation Italian woman who treated me as her sixth son. I was a pallbearer at her husbands funeral.

There are still lots of names I remember well, but have no way to know how they have changed in the more than 60 years since leaving high school.

Despo Stavers, listed alphabetically, sat behind me in every class I ever took in high school. Her first-generation Greek parents owned Capital Restaurant on Philadelphia Street, only two blocks from Steiner's Market.

The star halfback on the football team, Charlie Zbur, the best natural athlete I ever knew, was a coal miner's son from Ernest, a small mining town about four miles north of town. The town was totally owned by the Rochester and Pittsburgh Coal Company. They owned the mines, the houses, the company store, the elementary school building, and they figuratively owned the employees and their families.

Tough, hard-nosed, fearless kids, many of them were good athletes, but Charlie was head and shoulders above anyone in our school, certainly in Indiana County and maybe in the state of Pennsylvania. He excelled in football, basketball, and track & field. Charlie burned through a full football scholarship at the University of Miami (Florida), then another one at San Jose State (California). Charlie reached for the stars and went to the sunshine, maybe being the first kid from coal mining town of Ernest to even visit those two sunshine-filled states. Last I knew about Charlie, he had somehow ended up in Detroit, Michigan, where he got into the trash-hauling business and became a multi, multi millionaire.

Don Fusina

At some point around 1960, I was working at WIIC-TV. Jack Delaney belonged to Highland Country Club and introduced me to Don Fusina, The three of us lived in Pittsburgh's North Hills. Cynthia and I had two young children, as did Don and his wife Rosanne.

Don and I had common interests and backgrounds – the same age, both of Italian heritage, both loved to cook. Just like me, Don loved his family, was a salesman, and loved the Pittsburgh Pirates and Steelers. Together, we also loved hanging out, cooking, drinking, laughing and playing with our families.

We lived in McCandless Township, on Olive St. Don and Roseann's house was on Doral Drive, about eight houses up the hill.

Our children arrived one after the other, one year apart. Donald Junior was first and oldest, then our son Michael, then their David, and finally our Amy. The four got along so well, played together, vacationed together, had so much fun together. I think they loved each other.

We parents, from both families, pledged that if either couple died in a plane crash, the other would take the kids.

Along with Jack Delaney, Leonard Stewart, Chip Baxter, and some other young people from North Hills, we spent a lot of time at Highland Country Club.

We pretty much raised our children together, as well vacationing often at the Jersey shore in the summer, and snow sledding together in the snowy Pittsburgh winters. We spent many holiday dinners together, tasting new recipes. It became a tradition that we spent New Year's Eve together.

I'm reminded of an example of how tightly we were as families - a letter that David Fusina wrote in a commemorative 60th birthday surprise party thrown by my children, in Albuquerque. The letter captured many of the feelings of the members of the two families:

> *"My fascination with Ron was heightened when my father and Ron were partners in a two-ball event at Highland. We were at the pool. Word came they had won their match and were next matched to play the Bopes. Now keep in mind that the Bope father and twenty-something son were the most feared and heralded golfing team at the club. My dad and his friend were going to play them. This was bigger than Augusta, bigger than the U.S.Open . . . this was the Bopes.*

And as the buzz was building, I remember looking up from the pool and seeing Ron and my dad come down the stairs to join us at the pool. I remember thinking that these were the coolest guys to ever walk down the stairs at Highland. Not only were they the best-looking dudes to ever walk down those stairs, but I knew them both and I was related to one of them. I knew then that I wanted to grow up and be just like that."

Soon after that event, I accepted the position of general manager of the TV station in Albuquerque New Mexico. Although now a couple of thousand miles away from the Fusina family, we kept in close contact and visited back-and-forth as often as possible. Most memorable were skiing trips, enjoying the Albuquerque International Balloon Festival, attending the NCAA Final Four, and eating fine, New Mexican food.

About a dozen years later, Don seemed to have some problems with his eyesight. Don's condition worsened and eventually was diagnosed as suffering with a brain tumor.

At this point, I was doing consulting work, traveling the country, and I would detour through Pittsburgh to visit Don and spend time with Roseann and the boys.

One of the saddest days of my life was losing Don, when he died in 1994. I still miss him - a vibrant, handsome, wonderful friend, who passed too soon. I will always love him like a brother.

Glenn Beckert

Glenn Beckert was a year behind me at Allegheny College and a fraternity brother at the Phi Psi House. We roomed together for a year at Allegheny. Glenn was a good friend and an outstanding athlete, starring on the basketball and baseball teams. He was eventually signed by the Chicago Cubs, called up from the minor league in his second or third year, when Kenny Hubbs was killed in a plane crash.

We kept in touch with occasional phone calls after graduation. He had a very good career of 10 to 12 years, and was voted All-Star before he finished his time with the Cubs.

At some point, after his pro career, Glenn was working at the Chicago Commodities Market, he stopped taking my calls.

Later, I heard from others, that he learned that I had married Cindy Brown, daughter of Pittsburgh Pirates GM Joe L. Brown. Being a Pittsburgh native and having played his high school summer baseball for the Little Pirates team, Glen had his heart on playing for that big-league team one day. But when the Pirates passed him up and my father-in-law did not try to trade for him, that was about the time he stopped taking my calls.

Stars in the Making

The following people were among those that I worked with, supervised, and mentored. It was wonderful that they were unaware of their potential. It was equally wonderful to help them discover it.

Archie Coupe

The management at WRGB-TV and WGY-Radio, in Albany/Schenectady may not have known what a gem they had in Archie Coupe. Or maybe he was too soft-spoken and modest to toot his own horn. But those soft-spoken, modest, caring, and sincere attributes placed him in star status at WIIC-TV in Pittsburgh.

It was 1974. I was named local Sales Manager and was looking for more sales people. There was a sincerity about his first interview that set Archie apart from other candidates. Beyond that were his handsome looks, strapping athletic build, and resume as a Colgate University football player. His modesty was displayed when he talked about sharing the backfield with Marv Hubbard. Archie allowed that Hubbard, who became an NFL player and four time All-Pro with the Oakland Raiders, was the more talented ball carrier of the two. We hired him.

Because Archie had experience selling broadcast advertising in the upstate New York market, he was assigned some significant accounts. Among them were two of our largest accounts, Thrift Drug Stores and Mellon Bank.

In his modest, understated manner, he became the favorite TV rep calling on these accounts. Both had tough buyers, who demanded superior attention and service. The magic of WIIC-TV getting high shares of their business, while having the lowest share of audience, was testimony that the seller was the difference.

The Mellon Bank account was handled by Bill Connley, a Yale University grad and member of that school's baseball team. Talking about sports was the link to long conversations with Connley, and it helped our station secure superior shares of Mellon's big budgets.

Archie's path to stardom was understanding that the key to trust and big shares was getting to know the needs of the client. With both Bill Connely and Don Driscoll at Thrift Drug Stores, Archie worked his way into the hearts of the clients and into big shares of their business.

Another example of his charm was the turnaround of the Marv Jacobson Advertising accounts. Marv was full of himself and liked people to know it. While the competitive stations tried to win Marv over by taking him out to play golf, Archie understood that the real key to large budget shares and everlasting relationships was the one he developed with the buyer and office manager, Evelyn Stone. Four decades later, that relationship still exists based on Archie's sincere caring.

Archie could have stayed a long time in the nation's #10 TV market, but love drew him back to his home and Ellen, the love of his life. Rather than selling broadcast advertising, he became the marketing manager of Sounds Great, a fledgling electronic retailer. Under his leadership, Archie helped build the company from a small, local store to a 17-store statewide chain. His marketing savvy allowed him to sell advertising, but also to use advertising well on TV, and he became a star in both fields.

Archie coupled Sounds Great with local non-profit organizations. That matching was a "win-win" proposition. If the organization and its supporters are demographically linked with the customer profile of a business, there is a natural affinity established. For the customer profile of an electronic retailer like Sounds Great, it would be natural to become a sponsor of a charity run or race. If the customer profile for a high-end jewelry store appeals to wealthy and older clientele, a natural sponsorship is for a classical concert or a lecture series by eminent college professors. If Habitat for Humanity wants support for a new house or home site, look for sponsors like home centers, hardware stores and lumber yards. Matching customer/supporter profiles is a basic marketing concept that Archie used well in his business ventures.

Chuck Self

At the age of eighteen, most of us felt that we knew everything in the world except what we were going to do with our life. As a freshman at the University of Missouri and a switch-hitting catcher on the school's baseball team, Chuck Self did not know, or understand, the path to the end of his freshman season.

He switched his major from "baseball" to communications, with an emphasis on broadcasting and sales. The curve balls he could not hit at plate kept coming in real life - and he hit many of them out of the park. While an undergrad, Chuck worked on the campus radio station KOMU. He loved the tasks, and made his next personal goal to graduate and find a job in broadcast television.

He secured an interview with Lexington, Kentucky's WKYT-TV, the highly respected rights-holder to the University of Kentucky basketball telecasts. He saw himself working as a sportscaster for his first job in TV. Another curve ball ... the interview with the news director did not work out, but a chance meeting in the reception area with the station's sales manager did. It was like a screaming double down the right field line.

I met Chuck when doing marketing consulting for WKYT-TV in 1983. Making a few calls together, it was obvious to me that this young man had future all-star written all over his engaging personality.

One of the opportunities of my consulting work was meeting and working with station salespeople and eventually helping some of them advance to better jobs, in bigger markets. In less than a year, Chuck and his new wife, Ann, left the 83rd-ranked Lexington market to San Antonio, ranked 31st.

Chuck's star shone even more brilliantly at KENS-TV, as he moved swiftly from local salesperson, to Regional Sales Manager, to National Sales Manager - all in less than five years.

In those years in Texas, Chuck and Ann had two children and built relationships in the community – beginning their work with non-profit organizations that lasted their entire lives. Both Ann and Chuck had strong spiritual foundations and thrived in leadership roles with Big Brothers/Big Sisters, while he and Ann were the Youth Directors at their local United Methodist Church. Clearly, Chuck had discovered many ways to make it home.

Chuck's light attracted an offer to co-own a station in Jacksonville, FL. Three years there allowed Chuck to grow both professionally and personally, partnering again with Ann to lead and serve local non-profits. Working at broadcast facilities, in markets big and small, provides wonderful platforms for service-oriented station people to match up with non-profit community service organizations.

Chuck and Ann took fullest advantage and gave generously of themselves.

In Jacksonville, Chuck got an easy pitch to hit when Rick and Dee Ray, the heads of Raycom Sports, arranged for another well-earned opportunity for Chuck to shine, and get back on the first team in the sports field.

Chuck traveled the country helping Raycom Sports grow, building his reputation as a recognized service-oriented sales representative. All the marketing skills he has been honing at his earlier TV station jobs worked well on the national syndication front as well. As VP of Sales & Distribution at Raycom, he sold college football and basketball games throughout most of the country, to local television stations.

Working in Charlotte with Raycom, Chuck became involved with KAIROS Prison Ministries, which aims to address the spiritual needs of incarcerated men, women, youth, and their families. This is a volunteer mission unlike the local little league or library organization. This is a ministry that helps those on the inside, and changes those coming from the outside, allowing them to learn that we are all brothers and sisters. As Chuck and Ann have learned, community volunteering serves those providing the service as well as those being served. Chuck also got involved with the Cystic Fibrosis Foundation while in Charlotte and put together "A Room at the Inn" for local homeless people, at his church.

As Chuck was finishing his seventh year with Raycom, he got the call up to the big league. Warner Bros. Television is the production arm of Warner Brothers. Chuck become the highly successful face of Warner Brothers for the TV stations across 13 states, as Vice President of Sales for the Southeast.

Chuck, still a youngish, vital, and caring person, has now settled in a simpler life, as a successful real estate broker in western North Carolina. He continues to rely on the same relationship-building and marketing skills that served him well in the local TV industry, the national syndication business.

Chuck's star would shine in any world. I am grateful to have known him.

Debbie Bryant

Adventure, not resume-building, was her passion. So, as soon as Debbie graduated from the University of Kansas, she bought a one-way ticket to Puerto Rico where a friend had invited her to stay.

After working that summer as a temporary assistant to the production manager at the Timex factory in San Juan (a significant transition from being a student growing up in Kansas) Debbie was hired as an assistant to the owner of an advertising agency, where she learned to write "copy" and press releases.

Two years later, Debbie bought a one-way ticket from San Juan to Barcelona, Spain, where she found a part-time job as contributing editor to a bilingual pharmaceutical journal, and taught English as a second language.

After five years living abroad, Debbie was ready to head home to

Kansas City, where she was hired as a health science writer at the University of Kansas Medical Center. She worked hard and learned quickly. After winning an award from the American Medical Writers Association, she was hired as a medical copywriter at Ketchum Advertising in San Francisco. When I met Debbie in 1980, she had married and moved to New Mexico for her husband's job.

She was bi-lingual, smart, and sassy in a very charming way. Since we at KLKK had virtually no Nielsen ratings to show our worth to local advertisers, we needed a creative person like Debbie to draw attention to the new TV station in the market. She proved herself quickly - coming up with clever on-air and newspaper ads that won several awards from the New Mexico Advertising Federation. She also provided great energy and ideas for station programming and events. She was a star, without yet knowing it.

For the next 20 years, Debbie went on to hold multiple positions in broadcast television in three markets, including Los Angeles. Her last job in TV was Southwest Regional Manager for the quickly growing Telemundo Television Network. Here, she led the top-performing network sales office, producing an average of $16 million a year in advertising revenue for the network and its 63 affiliates. She managed a 10-person team based in three markets.

But by 2000, Debbie desired a more meaningful way to make a living. She packed her sports car with camping gear and traveled aimlessly through the Southwest on a three-month walkabout. This experience resulted in, literally, a miraculous series of events culminating with an offer to become the director of philanthropy for The Nature Conservancy of Texas, a dream-come-true for her.

Debbie was passionate about conservation and had been a devoted member of the Conservancy, but didn't realize that the Texas state chapter's offices were located in San Antonio, where she lived. Furthermore, she didn't imagine she might possess skills that would be valuable to the organization, but she did. Her mystical path to a position with the Conservancy was later described in chapter six of *What Should I Do with My Life*, by Po Bronson. Po interviewed over 900 people for his book, and only four had undergone a mystical experience that led them to a new career.

In 2001, Debbie oversaw the completion of a $60 million capital campaign. Eight years later, she became Assistant Vice President for University Advancement at Trinity University, in San Antonio ,where a $127-million capital campaign was nearing a successful close. But after her first year at Trinity, a new president was hired who, in turn, brought in a new VP for University Advancement.

Now Debbie found herself daydreaming about where and how she would like to end her career. She thought to herself, "I have one more fundraising position in me. Where do I want it to be?" The answer came swiftly: the Georgia O'Keeffe Museum in Santa Fe. Debbie had admired the artist for decades, read every book about O'Keeffe she could get her hands on, attended O'Keeffe's retrospective show in 1988 at the Los Angeles County Museum, and visited the O'Keeffe Museum in Santa Fe several times.

Debbie immediately went to the Museum's website and found out they were looking for a major gifts officer, which was her specific area of expertise in the complex world of fundraising.

Once again, through a truly miraculous series of events, Debbie was hired a few months later, not as a major gifts officer but as the Director of Museum Advancement at the O'Keeffe. In her first year, she led her team to achieve 112% of its operating revenue goal, which was over three times the contributed revenue from the previous year. Within 18 months of her arrival, the number of major donors to the museum had increased 100%. Debbie also wrote and produced the case statement for a $70-million capital campaign, and launched the silent phase of the campaign.

But despite her success, Debbie and the museum director viewed the world through entirely different lenses, and she decided it was time to retire. Today she continues to live in Santa Fe in her dream home, with her dream partner, doing all the things she loves while volunteering with multiple organizations.

Sarah Smith

From selling shirts and ties in Dallas, to a powerhouse broadcast company in Kansas City, Sarah Smith was among the rising stars I met before they recognized their own potential.

Sarah was fresh out of college and was discovered working in a men's wear shop by Jim Moroney. Jim was born with a silver rate card in his crib, being the son of the owner-manager of The Belo Corp, which owned several TV stations and newspapers.

Moroney was learning the business in the trenches, as General Sales Manager in the Belo-owned TV station in Tulsa. He saw this fiery, self-assured, attractive, and smart new college grad selling to "shirt and tie" type businessmen. He knew she could sell TV advertising to older business owners at his station in oil-rich Tulsa, and encouraged her to try TV sales instead of blue shirts and polka dot ties.

I met Sarah when she was a fledgling sales account executive with KOTV-TV, the CBS affiliate in Tulsa, OK. The year was 1986, and the two-Belo owned stations were clients of Noll & Co, which I represented.

Following some successful years at KOTV-TV, and a couple of ladder-climbing stops, Sarah went on to work for Belo at their ABC affiliate in Austin, as General Manager. In spite of having the backing of her own GM, Belo passed her over when more than a few general manager jobs opened at other Belo stations. Not to be denied, she said "goodbye" to the company she once loved and flew off to northern California – Chico/Redding/Eureka, TV market #132. Her star flared brighter there, and her confidence and drive kept growing.

Sarah may have remembered one of the mini-lessons I taught to people who were frustrated by trying, and trying, and not making progress. When it is time to try something different, bold, or drastic, always remember, "You can't fall off the floor."

Sarah was introduced to the Hearst Television Group VP of TV Sales, Kathleen Keefe, who hired her in Omaha, a forty-market jump from the Bluestone stations. She was hired as President and General Manager at KETV Omaha. Sarah kept a good friendship with her former Belo mentors. At the same time, she hoped they recognized they had missed out on her enormous talent and energy.

Before leaving Omaha, Smith served as president-elect of the Nebraska Broadcasters Association and was named Broadcast & Cable Magazine's General Manager of the Year in 2010, for markets 51-plus.

To recognize her work and take advantage of her enormous talent, Hearst elevated her to Kansas City's two-station facility. "Under Sarah's leadership, KETV has achieved outstanding results," said Hearst Television President/CEO David J. Barrett. "The station is Omaha's local news leader, with an outstanding reputation for journalism excellence and service to the community. And KETV's consistently strong revenue and profit performance attests to her impressive business credentials. We are confident that she'll be another outstanding leader for KMBC-TV and KCWE-TV, working with our talented staff to build on our long- standing legacy of leadership and service to the Kansas City community."

In Kansas City, Sarah leads a talented staff as community leader, supporting and promoting many local area non-profit organizations. Their success at marketing the station includes a place for Kansas City-area charities to share the stories of their talents and resources to lift those marginalized in the area. As a leader in the sometimes-glitzy TV business, General Manager Sarah Smith works to uplift all members of the community by supporting non-profits, all the while thanking her lucky stars for all the wonderful people she has worked with along her journey.

Sharon Norris

Unlike many of the rising stars I've encountered in broadcast sales, Sharon Norris never became a manager, never left for another market, and never wanted to be the boss.... of anyone but herself and her account lists.

I first met Sharon in 1982, after I had been fired by the owner of KLKK-TV, where I was General Manager for two years. While building a consultancy, I was asked by Arrington Art & Advertising agency to help manage the New Mexico McDonald's account. They needed someone who could deal with the television media for one of the largest billing accounts in the state.

When dealing with the Albuquerque TV stations, one of my tasks was to gather station availabilities, rating information, and costs, then propose advertising schedules and promotional opportunities. The market's leading station was KOAT-TV, the ABC affiliate.

Invariably, when trying to gather information from this power-house station, I failed to reach the sales rep on the account and would deal with the sales secretary, Sharon Norris. Also invariably, Sharon would provide the information I needed in an accurate, efficient, and professional manner. In countless encounters, Sharon came through - KOAT-TV got the lion's share of the budget, the sales rep got the commission while Sharon, the sales secretary, handled all the paperwork, discrepancies, and make-goods.

After months of seeing this happening again and again, I suggested that she consider becoming a salesperson. Her response, "They won't hire me; they already have a token female on the staff." I persisted with my encouragement to try to get her to seek the well-deserved position of sales executive.

After spending six months bugging her sales managers and the station's General Manager, the gruff and grouchy Max Sklower threw the Yellow Pages book to Sharon and barked, "Here, this is the biggest list at the station."

Out in the ad sales arena, Sharon was successful gaining new business accounts. With each new sale, she appeared in the doorway of the GM's office waving her sales contract, "I got another new account."

Before too many months, Sharon had an impressive list of existing accounts. Within a few years, she became the #1 biller for the #1 station in town. On her list were the top advertisers in the market. Principals at those accounts insisted that only Sharon Norris would manage their account, if the station expected the same outsized billing figures.

The more she sold, the more the management would cut her list, or her commission rate, or both. Sharon only redoubled her efforts and her billing with each cut. Eventually, the lack of respect from management caused Sharon to entertain conversations to switch employment to the CBS affiliate. KRQE-TV13 had lower ratings and billing, but had management that appreciated excellent work and were willing to pay her for the outstanding performance.

KOAT-TV not only lost their top biller, but they also lost major shares of the top accounts that Sharon took with her. After 15 years working at KOAT-TV, she switched her business card to KRQE-TV and, within a short time, became the market's top biller despite being a lower-rated TV station.

Sharon Norris proved that customer service, superior attention to customer needs, and caring about the advertisers' success were more important than having the highest ratings.

During the time at both TV stations, Sharon involved herself with the community, by serving on the boards of directors for both the Ronald McDonald House and the Albuquerque United Way. Her outstanding skills and understanding of marketing strategies paid off for her employers as well as the non-profits she served.

Never a manager at either station, but always an expert manager of her account list, Sharon had no interest in sales management. She certainly could have been a TV sales manager. Her passions were: working hard for her clients, making as much money as possible, and the care and support of her family. She was a super star in a different galaxy.

Tom Durney

Among the rising stars was one who stayed with us only a brief period. His reason was so strategic that it was totally understandable. He sold well for our station; I was able to help him grow, and we became life-long friends.

It was 1974. Tom Durney came to WIIC-TV from KQV-Radio in Pittsburgh. When that station was sold, he began looking at other options. Tom had the instinct and curiosity to learn more about television. He came as a seller, which he immediately did very well, and absorbed as much as we could teach him in our one year together.

Being mindful, Durney knew radio was his passion and true love. Others in the radio business already knew of his talent and they soon came after him with job offers, after his one-year education in television.

Wanting to stay in touch with this future super-star was important to me. But, to do so, I had to change his place of residence in my address book many times over in the next two decades, as he blazed through a galaxy of station owners and markets with the grace of the Greeks, the earliest astronomers.

From Pittsburgh to Syracuse, to Kansas City, then to Hartford, New Orleans, Denver, Washington, DC, Indianapolis, Greenville SC, back to Kansas City and eventually returning to Greenville, where he now is retired. This is not the resume of a man who could not keep a job, but rather, someone recognized as being an enormous talent - much in demand.

In the midst of these successful runs through markets, working for several ownership companies, Tom did what he did with me at WIIC-TV in Pittsburgh: learn quickly and contribute meaningfully. He absorbed all he could, recognized the bad practices that kept former owners, general managers, and sales managers from succeeding, and sprinkled some of the Durney stardust into the recipe for radio station success soup.

One of the most brilliant writers that I know, Tom authored a successful radio sales training program, wrote commercial copy, and designed ad campaigns for clients - just for fun and to help the success of his advertisers.

Tom Durney's success grew directly from his understanding that as a seller of a product, a service, or a concept, you must understand the needs of the prospect. He'd say, "To sell first, rather than listen first, is a formula for failure."

One of the things that Tom Durney loved so much about radio was its commitment to charitable organizations and causes. Radio stations used to air thousands of Public Service Announcements (PSA's) every year. In addition, stations would adopt certain charities or causes, and create on-air promotions drawing attention to the causes and generating donations. Durney loved to come up with promotional events that educated the public about the charity or cause, solicited donations, and endeared radio stations to their listeners.

Tom and his angelic wife, Amy, are approaching their Golden Anniversary. In all those cities that they traveled to together, raising four children, and eating pizza across the land, they discovered that Bellacino's Pizza & Grinders to be the best.

As a last act in his colorful and successful career, Amy and Tom have developed a successful restaurant chain in Greenville. Again, they know their customers and succeed based on the lessons learned in his broadcast career. I stop for a slice every chance I can.

seek PEACE.
give SERVICE.
be HAPPY.

seek PEACE.
give SERVICE.
be HAPPY.

TESTIMONIALS

seek PEACE.
give SERVICE.
be HAPPY.

Frank Thompson

Former Superintendent, Oregon State Penitentiary
Salem, Oregon

Before meeting Ron, during much of my career in law enforcement and corrections, I was in favor of capital punishment. In Arkansas, where I oversaw a prison, I began to doubt the value of state-funded executions when the state botched an attempt to kill an inmate.

By the time I met Ron in 2012, I had overseen the execution of two Oregon prisoners who had requested a speedy death and given up their appeals. That experience: setting up a new protocol for executing someone by lethal injection, constructing an improved death chamber, training my staff to assist the execution, and then witnessing those two men die, was deeply disturbing to me, and I retired 12 years later still carrying that burden.

I joined Oregonians for Alternatives to the Death Penalty shortly after Ron took over as its chairman. Ron was relentless in pursuit of the death penalty repeal. That's what it takes, relentlessness, to add or remove something from the state's Constitution. Ron was highly organized, effective, and respected. Under his guidance, Oregon enacted laws that all but eliminated the death penalty.

While my appreciation of Ron as a leader grew, his friendship became very valuable to me, both on and off the "capital punishment stage." Finding real, genuine friends is hard enough. In the fight to abolish the death penalty in Oregon, I found in Ron a devoted, faithful, and loyal friend that would support me through all kinds of challenges. We have become supportive of one another in our personal lives.

Having someone you can connect with and bond with is a lasting life experience. Ours is the kind of friendship that will stay with me during every storm, every struggle, and every hurdle in my life.

Frank Thompson

Letter from Sister Helen Prejean

Ron told me one time that I was his inspiration. He said he only became passionate about abolishing the death penalty after seeing me speak at a fundraising dinner in Albuquerque. It was at a transition home for men just released from prison, where Ron volunteered, cooking meals for the men and then sitting down with them to share.

Well, turn around is fair play. Ron's abolition work in New Mexico and Oregon has been an inspiration for me, too. A lightning rod can't generate its own juice, and I have been revitalized again and again because of the work of people, like Ron, whose tireless advocacy in state after state has us, as a nation, on the brink of a national death penalty repeal.

Abolition is a bigger lift in Oregon than most other states, simply because the death penalty is still embedded in the state's constitution. Under Ron's leadership, despite the odds, Oregonians for Alternatives to the Death Penalty has reduced the chances of capital punishment there to almost zero. Death row no longer exists. The death chamber has been removed. And the number of crimes for which someone can be charged with a capital offense has been reduced to four!

In addition to having admiration for his skills and accomplishments as a leader, I must say that I have come to deeply appreciate him as a friend. A humble and deeply devoted man of faith, I was struck by his use of the word "peace" in all his email and written correspondence. When I asked him about that, he laughed and said it was more a reminder to himself to be peaceful than advice for anybody else.

When Oregon's death penalty is finally repealed, I'm certain that Ron's name will be among those credited. I'm happy that he has received public recognition for his efforts, winning the 2023 Peacemaker Award in Salem.

Helen Prejean, CSJ

Paul J. De Muniz

Oregon Supreme Court, 2001 - 2012; Chief Justice, 2006 -2012

It was toward the end of my judicial career that I first met Ron Steiner at Queen of Peace Church. At that time, I learned of his dedicated leadership of Oregonians for Alternatives to the Death Penalty (OADP). Before becoming a judge, I had successfully defended a number of death penalty cases and understood that the application and imposition of Oregon's death penalty was arbitrary, random, and discriminatory. In addition, those serious legal concerns were reinforced by the Catholic Church's antipathy toward the death penalty. However, as an officer of the court and eventual leader of Oregon's judicial branch of government, I continued to honor my judicial oath to enforce the law, including the death penalty, despite my own beliefs.

As I got to know Ron, my understanding and appreciation of his steadfast commitment to ending Oregon's death penalty caused me to examine my conscience and attitude about the death penalty. Soon after my retirement from the court, I decided to accept his invitation to speak at an OADP fundraising dinner, to publicly express my own legal and religious opposition to Oregon's death penalty. In retrospect, it was his dedicated leadership in opposition to the death penalty that inspired me to begin publicly expressing my own opposition.

Ron's organization of the OADP Summit, bringing together leading opponents of the death penalty from different spheres of government and segments of Oregon society, proved to be the key event in OADP's opposition history. The Summit facilitated a successful legislative strategy that, in 2019, significantly limited the crimes for which the death penalty could be imposed—for the most part eliminating the application of the death penalty in Oregon.

That legislative success provided the rationale for the Oregon Supreme Court's 2021 decision in the David Ray Bartol case, concluding that the imposition of the death penalty for aggravated murder (under prior law) now violated the Oregon constitutional prohibition of disproportionate punishments. The court's analysis in the Bartol case made it likely that every previously imposed death sentence was likewise unconstitutional. Consistent with that analysis, Governor Brown then cleared Oregon's death row, commuting the death sentences of the remaining 17 death prisoners to life in prison without parole.

When a history is compiled of Oregon's last 45-year tug-of-war with the death penalty, OADP's name will be mentioned as the leading voice in favor of abolition.

Ron's dedication to peace, humanity, and love of fellow man has been an inspiration to me and so many others. His life has made Oregon a better place.

John A. Kitzhaber, M.D.

Oregon Governor
1995-2003; 2011-2015

I can't exactly remember when I first met Ron Steiner, but after meeting him, I knew I would never forget him. Our paths crossed after I issued a reprieve on the execution of Gary Haugen, in 2011, and declared a moratorium on the death penalty in Oregon. I immediately recognized Ron for the extraordinary individual he is - focused, compassionate and, most of all, dedicated.

His steadfast and principled leadership of Oregonians for Alternatives to the Death Penalty has been an inspiration to watch. This is not an easy issue. Capital punishment elicits deep emotions in people on both sides of the question. Yet Ron has displayed the rare ability to interact with supporters of the death penalty with a grace, respect, and patience that has won many over to his perspective.

I have rarely met a person with as much integrity and commitment to a cause as Ron. It has been a distinct honor to know him, and I am grateful for his tremendous service to our state.

I congratulate my friend Ron Steiner on receiving Salem's 2023 Peacemaker Award.

With Admiration and Gratitude,

Governor Kate Brown
Signs Senate Bill 1013 into Law

Above, the board of directors for Oregonians for Alternatives to the Death Penalty, witness the signing of Senate Bill (SB) 1013 by Gov. Kate Brown. Ron, on the left, front row, was the Chair of the organization for 10 years.

SB 1013 essentially did away with Oregon's Death Penalty. It reduced the number of crimes for which a person can be charged with a capital offence.

In 2021, the Oregon Supreme Court found that it was unconstitutional to hold a prisoner on death row when the crime for which he was convicted was no longer on the brief list of crimes punishable by death. Shortly after that decision, and just before leaving office, Governor Brown closed death row, transferred the men living there into the prison's general population, where they will live out their days, unable to receive parole. Then, Governor Brown ordered that the death chamber be dismantled, making it unlikely that the state will execute another person soon.

Governor Brown gave credit to Oregonians for Alternatives to the Death Penalty for "effectively ending the death penalty in Oregon."

2023 Salem Peacemaker Award Winners

Frank Thompson, left, and Ron on Oct. 18, 2023, just after receiving the Salem Peacemaker Award for 2023. The award is due to the men's dedication to repealing Oregon's death penalty.

Below is a link to the entire evening's presentation.
https://vimeo.com/876251145.

The introduction of Ron and Frank begins at the 7-minute, 43 seconds mark of the program.

seek PEACE.
give SERVICE.
be HAPPY.

EPILOGUE
by
Amy Halloran-Steiner
& Michael Ulku-Steiner

Philosopher and psychologist Carol Gilligan suggests that men naturally come to recognize the value of connectedness later than women. Forty years ago, while researching ethical decision making at Harvard, Gilligan realized that men tend to focus on independence and autonomy, whereas women care most about connecting with others. Gilligan saw value in both systems but asserted that 3,000 years of philosophy, written almost entirely by men, had undervalued connectedness.

In trying to re-value relationships, Gilligan often used the metaphor of a spider web. The more strands of connection, the stronger the fabric. The deeper the relationships, the richer the life. The more entwined and mutually dependent we are with families, friends, lovers, teammates, colleagues, neighbors, and fellow citizens, the more satisfying our lives become.

Our father spent the first half of his life excelling as a son, student, athlete, salesman, husband, father, and provider. He has spent the last half century expanding, extending, and redefining that success - building strands of meaning and purpose for himself and others as an entrepreneur, mentor, father, husband, friend, connector, man of faith, and activist for justice.

His path reminds us of the words of Albert Einstein: "The human being experiences himself, his thoughts and his feelings as something separated from the rest, a kind of optical delusion of our consciousness. This delusion is a prison for us, restricting us to our personal desires and to affection for a few people nearest to us. Our task must be to free ourselves from the prison by widening the circle of compassion to embrace all living creatures and the whole of nature in its beauty."

From Indiana to Meadville to Pittsburgh to Albuquerque to Salem and far beyond, Ron's creativity, responsibility, resilience, and generosity have sparked gratitude, learning, joy, and love in all kinds of people.

This book is the latest milestone in Ron Steiner's long and inspiring journey - building webs of care and connection, widening his circle of compassion and freeing himself and many of us from the delusion of separation. We feel inspired by his example. We love him dearly. We celebrate that he continues to share his journey with all of us.

seek PEACE.
give **SERVICE.**
be HAPPY.

www.ingramcontent.com/pod-product-compliance
Lightning Source LLC
Chambersburg PA
CBHW030529130626
46549CB00007B/3170